What others are saying about
"Sorty Makin' a Doctor"

"Coach Smith is Sorty a Doctor and Sorty a Coach. He pulls back the curtain to expose that he, like any of us doctors, are ordinary people that have an extraordinary calling. Being a doctor is not who he is or what we are, it is what we do. In a humorous and informative way, he tells stories of mentorship and commitment that would be necessary for the medical field or the basketball court. Many of us who pursued a career in medicine had no idea the path we were going, he gives an honest and spiritual dissection of the mission and professional calling and reveals the effort and tenacity necessary to succeed in medicine, coaching, and life."

Dr. Chuck Dietzen
Pediatric Physiatrist | Keynote Speaker | Award-Winning Author | Global Health Advocate | Motivator | Humanitarian

"I am impressed, that while working toward his degree, during his medical training, across different practice settings, and transitioning into coaching, Dr. Smith lived through some incredible experiences that he relates magnificently with humor and total honesty. God's hand in this transformation of Coach Smith's life is uplifting for all of us. Be Blessed and inspired!"

Kent Benson
President/CEO MKB Consulting, Former NBA Player, Collegiate All-American and National Champion

"An amazing chronicle that demonstrates the real truth behind medical education, medical practice, and the joy and heartache of being a doctor. This provocative look into the journey we call medicine revived a lot of memories and rekindled some long hidden emotions for me. This is an enthralling read that you won't want to put down."

Jeffrey C. Bird, M.D.
President Indiana University Health Ball Memorial Hospital/ Indiana University Health East Central Region

"Many people dream about what they would love to do and never quite get started on that path. Doug gives you an up close and personal look into how he actually took action on his dream. Sometimes that needed push comes from someone else's story. Enjoy Doug's journey from dream to fulfillment as he lays his out for you here."

Kevin Eastman
International Corporate & Sports Team Speaker, Author of *Why the Best Are the Best*, Former NBA championship coach and executive

"I have so much respect and admiration for Coach Smith's courage to make a massive pivot late in life and follow his heart. This book is such an enjoyable read!"

Alan Stein, Jr.
Author of *Raise Your Game: High Performance Secrets from the Best of the Best*

"A thoughtful reflection on the journey from a rewarding career in medicine to coaching a sport he's been passionate about since childhood. Dr. Smith offers a genuine reflection on the unexpected rewards that come from listening to your inner voice and following your heart."

Dr. Pete Temple
Author of *Playing In The Box: A Practical Guide For Helping Athletes Develop Their Mental Game*

"An entertaining, heartfelt and honest look at the power of walking away from one dream in order to fulfill another. From Dr. Smith's blue collar youth, to achieving his med school dream, to the trials and awakening he experienced in private practice, to his secret dream of coaching, this ultimate Indiana University basketball fan's journey is soul-baring, funny and 100% real. *"Sorty Makin' a Doctor"* reminds us that life is full of many chapters, and each of us holds the power to write the plot twist that allows us to ascend the next rung."

Daron K. Roberts, J.D.
Former NFL Coach, Keynote Speaker, Author of
Call an Audible

"Sorty Makin' a Doctor"

a memoir by

J. Douglas Smith, MD

There are three people in this world
who have loved me up and down, and
side to side, and I have loved them the same.
Laura, **Jeri**, *and* **Erin**
without you none of this would have ever
been possible; at least,
none of it would have been worthwhile.

Table of Contents

Foreword 9

Introduction 13

Chapter 1. Makin' a Doctor. 17

Chapter 2. College and Medical School 21

Chapter 3. We Finally Get to See Patients 33

Chapter 4. Fire 49

Chapter 5. Electives 55

Chapter 6. Internship 65

Chapter 7. Residency 75

Chapter 8. Private Practice—The Early Years 85

Chapter 9. Private Practice—Anderson 97

Chapter 10. "Sorty" a Doctor. 105

Chapter 11. How's Your Cargo?. 109

Chapter 12. Doing Life 119

    Home with No Call

    Moonsville

    The Running Ninja

    Teacher

    Last Call for Alcohol

    The Hound of Heaven

Chapter 13. Doctoring at Home 135

Chapter 14. Express Care 141

    Impostor

    Triage

    Fishing

    Glue

    Not Always Routine…Thankfully

    Plan for the Future

Chapter 15. Transitioning 161

Chapter 16. Hillary 173

Epilogue 183

Acknowledgements 195

Author's Biography 197

Foreword

Being a physician writer, I'm often honored with the opportunity to take a first dive into the manuscripts of other physicians who, like me, have decided to take a chance by opening their hearts and putting their life stories down in print. Some are motivated to tell a unique story through comedy or tragedy. Some have visions of writing the next great American novel. Others are compelled to draw attention to a situation that they believe needs activism, and sometimes they want to use the written medium to extend their professional influence to educate the public about a novel health threat, a new drug, a fad diet, or an imaginative scheme to fund healthcare.

Then there are those who just want to tell the stories of their lives and singular experiences. They want to leave something behind, a book on the shelf for the people they love — their kids, their families, and their friends. They hope to entertain and educate by detailing joys and heartaches experienced and lessons learned on the many paths walked and roads traveled in an individual lifetime.

"Sorty Makin' a Doctor" is that book. It represents a quiet journey of self-reflection in which Dr. Smith is able to answer his own question of "How did I get here?" It will be a reward-

ing journey through the eyes of a small-town family doc. Dr. Smith entertains and educates as he takes the reader through the maze of his memories from attending medical school, practicing medicine, and finally to becoming a basketball coach. We get a glimpse of the realities of this country, family doctor and the battles he faces with the changing currents of what it takes to be a doctor.

We all know a Dr. Smith, that person whose journey of self-discovery often finds him colliding with the brick walls of his own self-doubt. We see him taking punches that life deals along the way, but somehow always moving forward. We watch as he tries new things and embraces new opportunities. We hear him say as he looks back in the rear view mirror, "Yeah, I could have done that better," and we're inspired that he harbors no regrets. I am so glad that I got to work with that person, the Dr. Smith who wrote this book, for over twenty years.

In reading his memoir, I found myself feeling jealous. I'm longing for that peaceful yet active resolve, the sense that I have done enough. It got me thinking about my own game, perhaps it is even time for me to just dribble the clock out, take a final shot from the three point line, and call it a day.

Louis M. Profeta, M.D.
Emergency Physician, Public Speaker, LinkedIn Top Voice, Author of the critically acclaimed — *The Patient in Room Nine Say He's God*

Introduction

I have heard people say their professions or positions in life do not define them. I am here to tell you that for a long time during four years of college, four years of medical school, three years of residency training, and just under thirty years in the trenches of medical practice, my identity was tied up, part and parcel, with becoming and being a doctor. That totals about sixty-eight percent of my life, and I was dreaming of being a doctor long before I started college. I had a lot invested in that identity. I not only aspired to be a doctor. I wanted to be a really good one. For the most part, I believe that I was. I loved being a doctor, and as you will see, I also hated it. Looking back, if I could have eliminated half of the stress I put on myself, my medical career would have been much closer to the storybook tale I envisioned when I was young. Medicine was what I did, not who I was. It wasn't until the end of my career that I actually started to believe that.

As I reflect on this book about my life in and around medicine, I am struck by a couple of thoughts. First, although it did not always feel like it at the time, I was blessed to have participated in the delivery of health care to thousands of people over the years. I got to know many interesting people, and I hope I helped ease some of their suffering. Second, my story, while certainly unique to me, is no more compelling than the narrative anyone who has spent any amount of time in medicine could tell. Doctors see the results of the human condition with all that it entails, and humans are capable of and subject to more than most people can imagine. Wanting to get more than just a glimpse of humanity through a physician's lenses, my friends, the best a person could ever want, have encouraged me to share my own journey across this incredible landscape of clinical medicine.

Looking back over a career requires remembering, and recall is truly a funny thing. Some memories seem crystal clear. Others are a little murkier. As for the occurrences described in this book, they are reconstructed from the best of my recollection. While recreating these events may not be perfect, none are complete fictional fabrications. Names and descriptions of patients have been changed to protect innocent identities. That is the one dictate I always tried to keep in front of everything else. No matter what was going on, I believed my first duty was to care for patients. That meant paying attention to their emotional needs as well as physical and mental. In telling of the accounts in this book, I would never want patients to suffer any embarrassment. The initial maxim every medical student learns from the Hippocratic Oath is, "First, do no harm," and I still want to adhere to that.

Primum non nocere

That concept, first do no harm, is certainly good at face

value, but just like everything else, it can be taken to an unhealthy extreme. All the physicians I ever met wanted to help the people under their care, and they did not want to make any mistakes that might harm someone. Unfortunately, mistakes do happen even in medicine. For everyone except one person, I was able to extend grace and encouragement when an error occurred. Occasional miscues were expected and acceptable for my colleagues, just not for me. It took accepting grace from someone far more important than I before I was able to begin to forgive myself for a mistake. That almost paralyzing perfectionism as well as self-doubt, Impostor Syndrome, alcohol abuse, and a learned culture of honor in which I was constantly having to prove myself, were sometimes enormous obstacles to overcome. Despite these and many other challenges, I was able to have a very successful medical career, and I left under my own terms to pursue another labor of love.

In the pages that follow, I give life to the fulfillment of a farfetched dream for a boy from the wrong side of the tracks in Anderson, IN. The expedition includes heartache and joy, triumph and failure, tears and laughter. The human side of doctoring was not a straight path. For me, it had a few twists and turns, many ups and downs, and multiple lessons learned, some more easily than others. Through it all, one thing is for sure, it was never boring.

1

Makin' a Doctor

"This is my grandson. He's makin' a doctor."

Whenever I think of Ida Mae Smith, those are the words that pop immediately into my mind. Ms. Smith stood about 5' 4" feet tall, and she was almost as wide as she was long. She was a doting wife to a domineering husband for fifty plus years. She was the mother of four and a friend to many. She was my Granny. She always lived in Tennessee, and I always lived in Indiana. Both of my parents grew up in Tennessee. The joke in my hometown is that people from Livingston left there in the fifties searching for a good job in Detroit, but they ran out of gas in Anderson, IN. Luckily, factory work was plentiful in central Indiana until the late nineties. My father worked at GM/UAW. We took three or four trips a year to Livingston to visit my grandparents and other family members. If you have never encountered eyes that spoke of love, admiration, and pride for you, I feel bad for you. That is exactly what I felt every time I showed up at Granny's house. Even if my father dragged us in there unannounced at all times of the night, she would peer through the glass in the front door, and when she realized it was us, those hazel eyes would ignite in a sparkle that warmed me like melting butter. That look was always there, but as I advanced in college and especially after I was accepted into medical school, it exploded. That is when she started telling everyone she introduced me to what my career path was to be. She might even tell them twice.

I had terrible allergies as a kid. I was especially susceptible to the environment at my grandparents'. The trees, weeds, and animals hosted by the volunteer state, as Tennessee is known, always presented an all-out attack on my immune system. Frequently, my eyes would swell shut, my nose would stop up, and in that setting, I would have asthma. Granny also had bronchospasm, and she had congestive heart failure. So, we would often find ourselves sitting up in the middle of the night struggling to breathe. She would treat both of us…with rubbing alcohol. She would dab some on my chest and then some on her own. For reasons not completely understood, many respiratory conditions often improve with the transition from night into day. The two of us recognized that by our shared experiences. We would talk in wheezy whispers until morning would usher its welcome relief. Later, of course, I would discover that there were better treatments for our conditions, but somehow we managed to make it through some long nights together.

In the fall of 1982, I was deep into the first trimester of my first year of medical school at Indiana University. I sat at the table in her kitchen and studied for a Medical Microbiology midterm exam that I would be taking in a few days. Her funeral was the next day. I never got to tell her that I did well on that exam, that it was the one class in medical school in which I got the highest grade. I would not be able to tell her any of the stories and descriptions of a wonderful, awful life in clinical medicine. I think she would like knowing that throwing in a little love, as she did with the home breathing remedy, was often the best medicine. Heck, who am I kidding? She would enjoy hearing every stinking, last word. For now, here you go, Granny. Read this over somebody's shoulder, and we will talk about all of it in person someday.

2

College and Medical School

I can't remember when I first thought about becoming a doctor. In one of his songs John Mellencamp sings that "those old crazy dreams just kind of came and went." I can't say why that didn't happen to me. My upbringing was blue-collar, lower middle class, and our family could have been the poster presentation for dysfunctional. Like my parents, the people in our social circle were mostly migrants from the hills and hollers of Kentucky and Tennessee. A culture of honor, replete with the violence it permitted, even encouraged, tagged along when they moved north in search of work. I think my parents would have been proud to see me carry on those values and traditions. I know they would have been happy if I just stayed out of jail, graduated from high school, and went to work in the factories, but there were a few of my teachers who saw things differently for me. Sandy Pakes and Dick Resler at Washington Elementary School, Lillian Taylor at Southside Junior High School, and BC Smith at Madison Heights High School, each, in a different way, said, "You are a smart kid." Me! They were talking about me! I still remember Mr. Resler gave me a book to read. Really? I was supposed to read a book, and it wasn't an assignment for class? They were always encouraging me that I could "be somebody." Somewhere along the way, I started to believe them.

Except for teachers, the only professional people I ever interacted with were doctors. I saw that doctors dealt with science and interacted intimately with people, and I had discovered that I liked science and really loved people. So, that became the goal; I was going to be a doctor. I knew nothing about a doctor's life or what it took to become one, but that was the plan. One thing people said about me as I was going through school was that they admired my determination. What they didn't know was that it was actually stubbornness. If I said I was going to do something, I was damn well going to do it, or die trying.

Soon after coming to faith in my mid-forties, I was asked to give my testimony in church, on Easter Sunday no less. That's when I realized that stubborn determination, particularly back in those school days, was really an attempt to maintain some control in the midst of what often felt like chaos. When the turmoil of familial discord made the thought of studying a pipe dream, even if it meant staying up into the wee hours of the morning, I was unyielding in the pursuit of that "A." I was not going to allow that to be taken from me too. I think being Type A compulsive or a perfectionist probably comes to a person in multiple ways. Some of the tendency is probably in our genetic makeup, some of it is learned, and some, as it seems in my case, might be an unconscious coping mechanism. However this personality trait came to me, it helped and haunted me for a very long time.

Two semesters of typing kept me from vying for the highest distinction, from being the top student in my class at Madison Heights High School, and nothing could have mattered less. Looking back, if I had been valedictorian, I still would have spent the days in the summer after graduation cutting grass and painting bleachers for Mr. Bob Belangee, the Athletic Director at our arch-rival Anderson High School, and stocking shelves at Matthew's Grocery Store at night. I still would have gone to Indiana University. I only briefly considered one other school, and that was the United States Military Academy. I started through that application process, and I had word from the top aid to our venerable old Senator, Birch Bayh, that I was his leading candidate for an appointment. I don't think my dad's UAW ties were hurting me any there. Ultimately, my dad, a veteran of the war in Korea, was dead set against me going to West Point, and it was a terrible way to get to medical school. At that time, one had to complete his five-year hitch in the army after the Academy, then he could go on to medical school. I ended up only applying to IU, nowhere else. Later, I would not feel so bad for choosing a school for the love of its basketball team. Applications to Butler University skyrocketed after they made it to the national championship games back to back in 2010 and 2011. Is there a better way to pick a school?

I remember when my mom, brother, and neighbor drove me the two hours from Anderson to Bloomington to drop me off at college. To say that I was ill-prepared in emotional maturity to leave the nest is an understatement. We choked out our goodbyes, and I waved as they pulled out of the parking lot in front of Read Quadrangle there in the middle of the Indiana University campus. That was a lot of drama because I would be seeing all of them in just a few days. I was so insecure that for the first three weeks my mom would pick me and one of my high school friends, Marty Hall, up from school every Friday. We would stay home for the weekend. Then my poor mother would take four hours out of her Sunday to haul us back to Bloomington. As strange as it seems to me now, I think the unknown was more frightening than the known, even if that familiar environment was sometimes less than ideal. Finally, we had a home football game, and I stayed at school for the weekend. After that, I did not go home again until Thanksgiving.

For the rest of my college career, I would only return home for summers and holidays. I don't want to imply that I suddenly and magically matured overnight. Of course, I had not. What I did do is to turn into a Sunday through Thursday, hammer down, focused student, and the maturation process, the interactions in the social milieu of campus life, that occurred in that Friday to Sunday morning time-frame could fill a book, a very different book. If video had been as widespread as it is now, I have no doubt that my buddies and I could have easily filled an episode of Rob Dyrdek's "Ridiculousness." I know most of us are extremely happy that many of those escapades only live on in our collective memories.

With that template for my life, those college days flashed by like a thoroughbred at Churchill Downs. We won another basketball national championship under Coach Bob Knight. My fraternity claimed its first Little 500 victory. That four-man, fifty-mile bike race is the crown jewel in what has been called the "World's Greatest College Weekend." I was an alternate on that team. I didn't get to ride in the race. Still, claiming that victory was a pinnacle moment in my college experience.

Through all the four years in Bloomington, I did learn a few things, some of which came from the classroom. Mostly by the grace of God, I was able to survive and advance. You might recognize that phrase as one that is used to describe the goal in basketball tournament play. Sports really do represent a microcosm of life.

One afternoon late in the winter of 1982, my senior year of college, Mom called me. Back then long-distance phone calls required a toll, so we did not call often and mostly for emergencies or urgent matters only. I detected a quiver in her voice as soon as I answered the phone. Instant dread washed over me like steam off hot tarmac in August. She began to read a letter that had arrived there addressed to me.

"We are pleased to inform you that you have been accepted to attend Medical School at Indiana University..."

I was instantly relieved that nobody had died, and I honestly don't remember much more of the conversation that mom and I had. I believe that call was on a Tuesday, and I remember that my friends and I closed The Regulator down that night. So much for the four-day "hammer down" habit.

After I was accepted into medical school, it felt like I was back in the barbershop I went to as a kid where old men would tell their stories. I was in just the right place, but that relaxed, tranquil feeling didn't last long. When I arrived in Indianapolis to start medical school and met my classmates, I started to feel like I had a lot of catching up to do. Many of my fellow students had found ways to use the summer in pursuits that were at least somewhat related to medicine. I had poured beer.

Meadowbrook Pizza was and still is a neighborhood joint in Anderson. It is an institution with a devout cult following. Yes, it offers fantastic food that is not good for you, but it is the cold beer and atmosphere of camaraderie that draws people there. Strangely, the smoke crusted decor of gaudy beer advertisements around an ancient horseshoe-shaped bar in that dim and skinny room is inviting and even soothing. Patrons consider the place a blue-collar Cheers, and for the most part, it is a relaxing and peaceful place.

I had been going to Meadowbrook often since Christmas break of my first year in college. I got to know the owner well, so when I was looking for work that summer, he offered me a bartending job. I was grateful he didn't mention the fact that I had been coming into his place underage for the previous three years. I already knew most of the clientele. They were factory and construction workers, teachers and principals, sports broadcasters, newspaper photographers, firemen, GM executives, and just about every other class of working people, more men than women. Hard alcohol was not served there, only beer and very little wine. I didn't have to deal with mean whiskey drunks, but the generally calm environment I have described still had its moments.

Occasionally, when someone had too much to drink, I would have to cut him off. One afternoon as I got to work, Uncle Bob, as I came to refer to the owner, told me he had run a customer off earlier in the day. This particular gentleman had American Indian heritage. In the early eighties, political correctness was not much of a consideration, and this guy was known as Injun Joe. Sure enough, not fifteen minutes after Bob left, in came Joe, and he wanted a beer. After I explained that he couldn't be served any more that day, he just sat for a couple of minutes with his arms crossed, elbows resting on the bar with his head tilted slightly forward. Suddenly, he leaped to his feet, leaned over the bar, and at the same time he thrust an index finger into my chest, he let out this long, loud, primal screech. "I'm gonna keeeeeeeeeeeeeeel you!" Fortunately, his girlfriend calmed him down, and they just left. It took Bob's repeated reassurances over the next couple of weeks before I believed that I was not truly in mortal danger.

In the local pub, we see yet another example of how technology has changed our lives forever. A huge part of the culture in our little bar back then was the art of argument. People just liked to argue. Topics included just about anything — geography, history, politics, and of course, sports. Today those discussions go nowhere because someone will simply pull out his phone and retrieve an instant answer.

One evening, I finished the early bartending shift and walked around the bar to become a customer. I was sitting across from a man named Jimmy, who was a correctional officer at the penitentiary. He also had an unfortunate nickname that, surprisingly, he seemed to enjoy. Fat Whore was not known to back down from an argument. That night, he and I got into it, and I can't for the life of me even remember what it was about. It was rare that a disagreement would escalate beyond a little shouting, but on this occasion, Jimmy wanted to beat me up. The collective good sense of the bar intervened. I was not going to be dragged outside, but all agreed that we had to have a way to settle our disagreement. On a shelf under the corner of the bar, there was an old jar of pickled jalapeño peppers. That was it. Fat Whore and I would have a pepper eating contest. Best man wins. With red, tear-streaked faces and snot dripping from our noses, we called a truce at thirteen apiece. The next day, when it was time to move my bowels, I learned there are many ways that one pays for his poor decisions.

Memorable as they were, I just didn't think the experiences I had at Meadowbrook were on par with the resume-building endeavors my classmates described. Some had worked in doctors' offices and hospitals. Some had done research. I had dripped snot with Fat Whore and nearly got my ass kicked by Injun Joe.

More doubt flooded my mind when I was actually standing in one of the registration lines on the first day of medical school on the Indianapolis campus. I was floored when I saw Dr. Robert Naviaux standing beside me. At the time he was just Bob. He had been the graduate lab assistant in a couple of the advanced biology courses I had taken as an undergraduate. I had correctly estimated him to be an intellectual bad-ass. At IU Bloomington, the biology and chemistry classes had lecture halls that were busting at the seams. Especially early on, I worried that I could not keep up. Now, Bob Naviaux, an instructor in some of those classes, was in my medical school class. I was going to have to compete with him and three-hundred other people I surmised to be in his league. I knew they were Division 1, and I was barely intramural. Insert your own expletive. I had too many that would be way too offensive for even a modestly sensitive person. What the @#%# had I gotten myself into?

The pace of the next two years, particularly the very first trimester, was frenetic. It was the Indianapolis 500 to the Sunday pleasure drive I was used to. When I arrived in Indy, I had decent handwriting. By the time the first set of classes was over, I had my own shorthand scribble that only I could decipher. Yes sir, I was fulfilling the first obligation of becoming a doctor.

God had me on the late physical maturation plan. I was still as skinny as a beanpole when I started in Indy. I shared an apartment with my friend and study partner from college, Bret Henricks, who is now a radiologist in Lakeland, FL. He was on a Navy scholarship that covered his med school tuition as well as room and board, and I was bat-shit poor. We would usually go to the supermarket together on Sunday. Bret would be pushing his cart brimming with different varieties of beautiful, real food. Most weeks, I didn't need a cart. I carried a pack of baloney, a loaf of white bread, and a few twenty-five cent packs of macaroni and cheese. That would be it until the next Sunday. Bret was willing to share, but I was mostly too proud to ask. I lost weight that I didn't have to lose. My family would whisper behind my back when I went home. "Is he sick?" they would ask. I wasn't sick, just a little hungry.

Between the first and second years, Bret went to Newport, RI for his navy training. Before he returned, I moved back to Mom and Dad's house in Anderson. I would have to commute a little over an hour each way, but at least I would be able to eat. That summer, Uncle Bob would gladly have given me the opportunity for an encore at Meadowbrook, but I worked in Dr. Randy Rosenthal's gonorrhea laboratory instead. As disgusting as it sounds, it wasn't a bad way to spend the break from classes, and since somewhere in the neighborhood of 580,000 Americans contract "the drip" in any given year[1], I perceived a sense of importance in what I was doing. I just felt like I needed to shower three times a day while I was doing it.

Like the time in Bloomington, the first two years in Indy passed in a blur. Medical microbiology, biochemistry, anatomy and physiology, embryology, histology, pharmacology, pathology, and a general introduction to medicine were

---

1 https://www.cdc.gov/std/stats18/default.htm

among the courses attacked and, more or less, conquered. The Friday and Saturday "out for bedlam" lifestyle was tempered but not completely eliminated. Sometimes I would squeeze the life out of my paltry food allowance to go to the bars with Bret. My friend and fraternity brother, Mark "Taz" Kemper, who graduated a year before I did, was already working and making good money. Many times he would pick me up, and we would go for food, drinks, and frivolity slightly less raucous than we had previously been used to. Taz always paid with a credit card, running a tab at the bar. He never asked for anything in return. I still haven't repaid him. I have tried to tell him, but I don't think he will ever truly understand that those respites were absolute life-preservers in what could have been a sea of drudgery.

3

We Finally Get to See Patients

We had little contact with patients during those first two years, and when we did, I really did not set the tone for the start of an excellent clinical career. First up was learning to take a medical history. Getting accurate and useful information from patients and their families is truly an art. It definitely takes some time to develop that skill. The first real patient I interviewed was a patient on a general medical floor at Wishard Hospital. Wishard was the Marion County hospital for impoverished patients. The Whiz had a reputation for making or breaking green students. Fortunately, my patient was a congenial gentleman. He was in his mid-thirties. I ascertained fairly quickly that his chief complaint was cough with sputum and fever. He was hospitalized for the treatment of pneumonia. The next part of the history is what is referred to as the review of systems. We ask a comprehensive set of questions about every body system. For the cardiovascular system, a few items we would ask might include questions about chest pain, racing heart, and shortness of breath when lying down. The gastrointestinal system might be covered with abdominal pain, vomiting, constipation and the like, and we proceed down a list. My preceptor for that interview was a psychiatrist. She was overseeing a group of about five of us who had been scattered to different patient rooms. She sat in for a short while with each of us. Her feedback to me was that I listened to my patient very well, but that she wanted to kick me in the shins because I was so stinking slow. Fortunately, she was not present for the end of my discussion with this man. I had dutifully covered the neurological system in his review of systems. Headaches? — no. Numbness or tingling? — no. Weakness? - no. He had been sitting up in bed, covered with a blanket to his chest. As I got up to leave, I commented on his physical stature. He looked very muscular in the upper body. Just to finish with polite conversation, I asked if he exercised regularly. He replied, "Since I got paralyzed, not too much." This gentleman who had been talking with me for forty-five minutes was paralyzed from the waist down, and I didn't have a clue. I only discovered the most important part of his medical history by happenstance. I was just glad the shrink, who seemed to have an inclination toward corporal punishment, had not been present for that part of the interview. If she had heard that exchange, she might have wanted to kick me in the nuts.

The only other patient experience that I remember before third-year clinical rotations began was when I was shadowing an older student. I had met Lloyd Lewis at IU Bloomington. He was two years ahead of me and agreed to be my student preceptor. That meant that about two or three times over the first year when schedules permitted I would get to follow him as he participated in one of his clinical rotations. One time when he was on an orthopedic rotation at Riley Children's Hospital, he invited me to observe a surgery with him. I was going into the operating room (OR) for the first time. The entire process seemed surreal to me. While changing into surgical scrubs in the locker area I felt detached as though I was looking down and watching myself get dressed for the first time. I watched as Lloyd prepped at the scrub sink, and the smell of that surgical disinfectant produced an unexpected result. It made me feel high. Albeit a little disorienting, it was not a completely unpleasant feeling.

The planned procedure was for a teenage boy to have some operative correction for scoliosis that caused his back to look, literally, like the letter "S." We entered the operating room, and with the aid of one of the OR Nurses, Lloyd got into his sterile surgical gown and gloves. I looked around in amazement at this sacred environment, and suddenly I actually saw the patient. There was this frail and pale-looking teenage boy lying naked face down on the operating table. The anesthesiologist had just put him to sleep, and the nurses were getting ready to scrub his back. After that, a sterile surgical drape would be placed over him. Only, I never saw that part. I suddenly felt overwhelmed with how this kid was lying there abjectly vulnerable. The lights started to blur and it seemed like the ceiling was moving away from me like a rapidly ascending elevator. I passed out, before the operation even began. The next thing I remember was waking up on a gurney outside in the recovery area. A nurse saw that I had awakened and offered me some orange juice. After a few minutes, she asked, "Are you ready to go back?" Back in there? Was she serious? She was, and with very little pomp and circumstance, she led me back to the entry area and redirected me to put on a surgical cap, and mask. The booties I had put over my shoes were still in place. Then she marched me in and placed me, standing behind Lloyd. "Your student is back," is all that she said. Lloyd was holding a retractor. He barely turned his head and said, "You OK?" One of the residents who was scrubbed in on the case said, "It happens." The staff physician never even blinked. He was laser-focused on helping that misshapen kid. I watched the rest of the procedure without incident, and nurses never had to lift my limp carcass off the floor again.

Botching a patient interview and taking a snooze from just walking into an operating room were foremost in my mind as I started my third year. The rest of my medical school experience was to be clinical work, and I felt like I had established a weak and wobbly foundation for myself. However, I wasn't able to wallow in self-pity or self-loathing. There simply wasn't time for it. From the first rotation on, the busy engine of life ratcheted up another couple thousand RPMs.

My first assigned course was Obstetrics and Gynecology (OB/GYN) at University Hospital. Almost all the patients, who were seen there, were private patients of prestigious staff doctors. Many of them were consulting for sensitive issues such as infertility. Because of that, the lowly students, I think there were four of us, were required to show up and spend each day reading in the hospital library. We did not have contact with our supervising residents often, but when we did see them, it made the day, at least it did for me. Dr. Kristina Box, now the State Health Commissioner in Indiana, was a resident on that service with us. Dr. Box was smart, witty, a good teacher, and to a young, single, and impressionable young man, she was easy on the eyes.

The busy part came because I was introduced to call. Every third night during that month-long OB/GYN rotation, I was required to report to Labor and Delivery over at Wishard. Being on call meant one out of three nights I would be up all night watching and sometimes helping with the delivery of babies. Wishard was an extremely high-risk environment for obstetrics because most of the mothers did not participate in recommended prenatal care. Often a mother's first contact with the medical system would be when she showed up in labor. These women, frequently just kids themselves, came from cultures of chaos, and their way of life did not stop at the door when they entered. Even more than its Emergency Department, Wishard's Labor and Delivery was the loudest and most emotionally intense environment I ever experienced. Since then, I haven't personally witnessed anything even close. The very first night, I think I watched and heard three deliveries.

The next morning brought new responsibilities for me.

The charge nurse informed me that it was my duty to draw blood for labs to be done on patients on post-partum (the area for ladies who had already delivered their babies) and the gynecology floor. I had only drawn blood one time before when a classmate and I got to practice on each other. That morning, the nurse said I was lucky, only three to draw that day. She handed me a bucket with supplies and a card with room numbers, patients' names, and the number and color of tubes of blood that were needed. At the first stop, I confirmed the room number and assignment three or four times. The rooms were on the second floor and numbered in the two hundreds. As I repeatedly checked the card the nurse had given me, my heart rate climbed to match the number beside that first door. It was about 5:30 in the morning. No light would be on in the room. I extracted a penlight from my lab coat pocket, gently knocked, and entered. The light did not provide the illumination I had hoped. In an instant, I was down, and the bucket and tubes were scattered over the floor. A light snapped on, and I immediately saw the cause of my calamity. Staring down at me with disheveled hair and a menacing grimace was one very large lady. My foot was entangled in the chain that shackled my patient, a prisoner of the Department of Corrections, to her bed.

She softened with grace when she saw me there.

"You a rookie, ain't you," she said as a declaration, not a question.

"Yes," I managed to croak feebly.

"Get over here. I gonna show you how to do this," she

ordered. She did indeed show me, and I was so grateful. This is probably the most obvious example of direct instruction I received from a patient, but a huge part of the medical knowledge I acquired over the years came from interactions with patients.

Maybe because it was the first, I seem to remember more about that rotation than most of the others. We also manned a gynecology clinic at Wishard once a week. I was working with the senior resident on the service at that clinic one afternoon. We examined another very large lady who had a gigantic Bartholin gland abscess—a large local infection on the vulva outside the vagina. We reviewed the treatment plan. I was to slice into that lemon sized lump and drain the pus. With the resident standing off to the side and slightly in back of me, I injected some numbing medicine in the skin overlying the abscess and then made a stab incision with a scalpel. Fortunately, I was young enough, agile enough, and had quick enough reflexes to duck and scoot out of the way fast enough so that the stream of putrid discharge that blasted out of that pus pocket hit the wall behind me and not my face. I wish I could recall the resident's name, but she was not Dr. Box. Her response was classic. With eyes opened wide, I looked up at her. She shrugged and said, "Good job."

The next rotations included Orthopedics and three months of Internal Medicine (IM). Then I moved on to a General Surgery rotation that was two months long. During the first month, I was on a vascular surgery and trauma team at Wishard. There were four or five students on that team.

We pre-rounded at 5 a.m. to have information ready and organized for the residents who met up with us at 6 a.m., so they could confer with faculty staff at 7 a.m. Then we held retractors during surgery for the rest of the day. When the cases were finished, we had post-op checks and new admissions to work up. We generally left the hospital between 8:30 and 10:00 p.m. There were no days off that month.

Vascular surgeons deal with the effects of diseases that clog up arteries. The resulting poor blood flow can lead to loss of body parts. I saw more feet and lower legs amputated in that month than I ever dreamed possible. We were so busy keeping up with the constant barrage of new patients that I don't remember what help was offered to those patients for the emotional toll those losses imparted. I know it was painful to see for them.

Through all of it, just as in the entirety of life, I was always dealing with personalities. After medical school, physicians in training are called residents. First year residents are interns, and those in their last year of training are referred to as senior residents. The people in the middle are designated by their year in training or simply junior residents. On that vascular surgery service, there was a senior resident, junior resident, and intern. The senior resident and interns were cynical people. The intern was particularly malignant. I recall the following year she was asked to leave the program, and I was glad to hear that news about her. Now, after years of caring for people and knowing that there are usually hidden reasons for boorish behavior, I hope she got some help and found happiness.

Midway through my time with them, they decided that my answers to their questions were too long-winded. For the last half of that month, I was permitted only to say "Good" or "Bad" when responding to them. For example, if a bedside chart showed that the patient had a fever, they would point at it, and I was only allowed to say, "Bad." Most of my clinical rotations would not have that same brutally exhausting schedule that we had on that service. Most of theirs did. (In 2003, the Accreditation Council on Graduate Medical Education placed stipulations on residents' workloads including a limit of eighty hours per week.[2]) Now, I get that by shutting me up, they were probably just trying to steal any minute they could for themselves. At the time, I felt like they were demeaning me personally. I played their game, but I wasn't happy about it.

The personality most memorable to me was that of Dr. James Madura. He was affectionately known as Mad Dog, not to his face of course. He was the faculty staff for my second month of surgery. That service was back at University Hospital. In contrast with the OB/GYN rotation there, students were very active on the surgery service. We saw every patient and participated in every surgery. Patients were referred for some of the most complex surgical conditions. Positions on his service were coveted by those who were pursuing surgical careers. I was placed on the A team by the luck of the draw. I could have just as easily ended up on the B team. There are a few reasons why I am glad I ended up where I did. First, and

---

2 https://www.ncbi.nlm.nih.gov/pmc/articles/PMC1169274/

I am not joking, the B team had a senior resident named Dr. Grimm, a junior resident named Dr. Gross, and an intern named Dr. Slaughter. I could not imagine meeting patients with that morbid group. Secondly, the other students on the A team were solid and fun to be around. While the hours were not quite as bad as over at the Whiz, we still spent a lot of time together. Most importantly, I would not have met Dr. Madura.

Dr. Madura had the temperament of a stereotypical surgeon. He was somewhat egotistical. He was impatient. He loved to teach and expected everyone to learn quickly. He demanded excellence from all, and I loved him. I used an elective my fourth year to have another month on his service. After my name was called at our graduation ceremony, I veered from the straight walk across the stage to go straight to Dr. Madura to shake his hand. At that moment, I knew that he loved me too-I saw it in his eyes, and I never saw him again.

You may not realize that there is a proper technique for using a pair of scissors to get them to cut properly. Dr. Madura had given us a two-minute demonstration and thoroughly expected that we would be proficient in that simple task. One time while operating with him, I was on the opposite side of the table, holding a retractor with my left hand and using scissors with my right hand to cut suture. When he or the senior resident, Dr. Bruce Van Natta, would tie a stitch, he would hold up the excess suture material and say, "Cut." My job was to cut the suture at the precise angle and length. For some reason, I could not get the scissors to cut without taking a few tries.

"Smith, that's a scissor, not a saw," Dr. Madura scolded me after the first time.

It happened again.

"That's a scissor. If you do that again I'm going to punch you," he said.

It happened again, and he reached across the patient and punched me in the center of the chest. It wasn't hard, but it did make a thud. A few minutes later, the scrub nurse handed him those same suture scissors because he was in a better position to cut for his senior resident. He found that the scissor was faulty and dull.

He said, "No wonder," and tossed them on the floor. As the nurse handed him a new pair of scissors, he looked straight at me. His eyes were twinkling, and I knew he was grinning behind his mask.

It was on his service that I witnessed one of the most horrific things I have ever seen. Our patient was in her late-twenties. She lived in a nursing home. She had been in a vegetative, comatose condition for several years. I don't remember what caused her problems. It might have been a traumatic brain injury. She received nourishment through a feeding tube that went through the outside skin into her stomach. We were seeing her because the contents of her stomach kept finding a way into her lungs, causing her to get pneumonia. We would be doing a procedure called Nissen fundoplication. The top part of the stomach was to be wrapped around the lower part of the esophagus (swallowing tube) to prevent her liquid diet from refluxing up into her lungs. When we opened her belly, we saw a mass in her pelvis. It looked to be the size of about a twelve-to-fourteen-week pregnant uterus. One of the obstetricians was called into the OR. She traced the fallopian tubes from the ovaries to the uterine mass, and then she placed a sterile Doppler, a sensitive instrument used to hear faint heartbeats, against the mass. Just as we all were dreading, we heard fetal heart tones. The mass in her pelvis was her uterus, and it housed a baby. She had been raped.

This debilitated, innocent soul had been violated in the most disgusting way imaginable, and the school and hospital did not want students to misrepresent anything about this case. We were coached to avoid the media completely, and that required considerable stealth because the campus was flooded with television news crews and reporters for days. I never heard whether anyone was ever apprehended and convicted for raping this poor, defenseless girl, and I don't know what happened with her health. This was the beginning of my recognition of one very unpleasant, yet undeniable, fact that years in medicine would reinforce regularly. Like it or not, evil does exist in our world.

Other rotations during the third year included Neurology at the Veterans Administration Hospital and Psychiatry (Psych) at Larue Carter Psychiatric Hospital. When we were on Psych call, we covered all the hospitals on the main campus. One evening, another student and I were talking with the resident after we had finished dinner at Larue Carter. We were called to see a patient in the Emergency Department at Wishard. When we got there, we were directed to a semi-isolated area that housed about half a dozen patients. Our patient was in his mid to late twenties. He had been brought in by ambulance with police assistance, because he had been "creating a disturbance." He was restrained with four-way leather restraints, lying on his back. As we approached, he was quiet. Just as we got to the bedside this creature with the wildest eyes I had ever seen sprang as far as he could manage against the restraints. It seemed like he came within inches of our faces. He bellowed, mostly gibberish. He was stuck on words that started with w. I made out warlords and wombats between the wailing and slobbering. I remember two times in my adult life when I nearly pissed my pants. One of those happened when I absentmindedly stuck my hand down in a horse-feed barrel where a 'possum was hiding, and the other when this gentleman ambushed us with that howl that seemed to have emanated from his earliest ancestors.

The resident calmly perused an old record that had been retrieved from archives. The patient had no identification, but some of the staff had recognized him. Medication was ordered, and a nurse returned with a syringe full of the antipsychotic medication, haloperidol. Now, we had to give it to him. The Psych team, two students plus the resident, and two other nurses held him down while the first nurse injected the medication into one of his thighs. As soon as the medication had been administered, the resident, our boss for the night, told the nurse we would be back in about twenty minutes. Really? That was it? We were leaving?

We went to a little waiting area that only had a couple of

people in it, and the resident answered pages he had received while we were wrestling with our patient. He then explained to us that the patient was known to have schizophrenia. He was having a full psychotic break. He would undergo a complete medical work-up once things calmed down, but likely he had just stopped taking his meds.

When we returned, his behaviors were the same but lacked about fifty percent of the ferocity. I think a slightly lower dose of the same medication was delivered in the same way. When we went back the next time, we encountered a subdued young man who was very contrite. His restraints had been removed. He offered effusive apologies. Earlier I had been distracted by thoughts of self-preservation, and I hadn't noticed what he was wearing. His garish pantsuit was adorned with red and black feathers, and it was twisted out of place, torn in places, and missing buttons. He tried to cover himself in modesty, and a nurse handed him a blanket as we left. I knew two things for sure: mental illness is real, and psychiatry was not in the cards for me.

The rest of third-year rotations went off with little fanfare. The only other excitement came again on Psych. I was back on call. Call is the place where all the great learning in medicine occurs, by the way. This time one of the residents and I were seeing a patient at Larue Carter. He was clearly anxious when we entered the room. We reviewed his history before we saw him. Like the gentleman at Wishard, he also had a long history of psychiatric problems, and he had been violent with providers in the past. I listened as the resident interviewed and talked kindly and soothingly to this man. Then I stuck my hand in my pocket and accidentally hit a button on my keychain. The Indiana Hoosier fight song blurted out of my pants, and our patient's anxiety turned instantly to overt agitation. I was at once embarrassed and afraid. I thought that if the resident, with her one hundred pound physique, could offer any assistance, we could probably take this guy. However, I had already witnessed the extraordinary strength one can harness when he is pursuing the just cause of defending the free world against wombats, warlords, and other demons. I also knew that having a physical altercation with a patient was not a great thing to have in my file. Fortunately, I was able to extinguish the sound quickly. Prior to the interruption, the resident had begun to develop some rapport with this guy. It took her some doing, but after a while she cajoled him back to a state of mere anxiety.

After a treatment plan had been established and agreed upon, we left this gentleman. When we got out of eyesight and earshot, she let me know just how stupid I had been. Unlike the psychiatry staff doctor who oversaw my history taking lesson, this resident did not say that she wanted to kick me, but it was clear that was an option she considered.

Over that one year, I witnessed human suffering that was beyond belief, and I saw a few miracles. I will always remember the first full "code blue" that I observed. Code blues, or codes, are depicted dramatically on television and in the movies. In real life, they do include pushing on the chest, putting in breathing tubes, and shocking hearts that have stopped, and they are almost as emotionally charged as the film industry likes to demonstrate. They just lack the foreshadowing, surreptitious looks between George Clooney and Carol Hathaway. I was on Internal Medicine at Wishard when I saw my first code. I was walking with one of my classmates on one of the medical wards. A code was called out on the overhead speakers, and we were nearby. When we got to the location indicated, the surgery team, who happened to be passing the area, was already in action. The person receiving everybody's attention was an established patient in the hospital. She was yet another very large lady, and she had just collapsed in front of a bank of elevators. Dr. Rosie Jones, a petite, first-year surgery intern, who became an accomplished general surgeon with a subspecialty in bariatric procedures (treatment of morbidly obese patients) was performing chest compressions. If not for the seriousness of the situation, that picture would have been almost humorous. The full code team arrived and took over the resuscitation. This lady survived to be whisked off to the Intensive Care Unit (ICU). About four days later, we saw this same lady standing and talking very loudly on one of the pay telephones near the place where she nearly died. She was clearly disciplining one of her kids. Mothers are tough.

The third year came to a close, and I, like most of my classmates, survived the rigors of those clinical rotations. We were prepared to advance to fourth-year clinical electives, and I had only suffered one punch in the process. Today, that punch could make headline news and possibly even end a surgeon's stellar career. For me back then, that jab didn't even count as a punch; it was just a love tap.

4

Fire

Medical students and doctors are not spared any of the joys, despair, thrills, and sorrows that non-medical people experience as they go through life. My sister gave my parents their first grandchild while I was in my second year at IU med. I missed my brother's graduation from high school because of third-year time demands. Holidays came and went more quickly than they ever had. Through it all, I gained a lot of new friendships. When you work through the furnace-fire of adversity created by intense intellectual challenge, frequent fatigue, and the emotional drain from seeing sick people, you cannot help but grow close to people who are having similar experiences. The support I received from my classmates and instructors, but especially classmates, was the gasoline that kept the engine running. I saw Tom Kirkwood, M.D., an old buddy, at a medical conference some thirty years after our time in medical school. He greeted me with the heartiest hug,

49

and we picked up right where we left off. Moments like those let me know that just as I had received inspiration, I had given some much-needed encouragement as well. We helped each other through. Sometimes one of us would just need a joke, a pat on the back, or a look that said, I know what you are going through. Sometimes a lot more was necessary.

My college buddy, Mark Kemper, saved my butt again. Commuting from Anderson while I had fixed hours during the second year was fine, but when the clinical rotations began my third year, that didn't work anymore. For some rotations, I would have been leaving Mom and Dad's at 3:30 a.m and getting home at 11:00 p.m. Mark lived in a townhouse apartment with another one of our fraternity brothers, and they were willing to rent me their extra bedroom for next to nothing. I was still strapped for cash, and this arrangement was much more affordable than what I had the first year. It allowed a bigger budget for groceries; I didn't have to worry about food.

In the fall, I was on an Internal Medicine rotation at Wishard, and as it occurred pretty frequently during that stage of our lives, another of our pals was getting married. We had prepared ourselves for the wedding with a few libations, but nothing extreme. The ceremony was nice. Louie and Renee tied the knot in the usual way, and we were heading to the reception. As we drove toward the festivities, we heard numerous sirens. The route would take us within a couple blocks of our apartment. As we drew near, almost in unison, the three of us said, "That's close to our place." When Mark made one more turn, we saw all the emergency vehicles in front of our apartment, and some smoke was still trailing out of all of the windows. Our apartment had burned.

Fortunately, the blaze was contained to our place. No one was injured. Our neighbors could continue living in their units, but ours was no longer habitable. Before the fire department realized we were moving about and kicked us out, I was able to box a few of my textbooks, bag a few clothes that were not completely covered with soot, and lament a busted Muhammad Ali decanter.

We didn't make it to the reception. My two roommates and I spent the night with yet another fraternity brother and his wife who lived in the same complex. Sleep hid from my anxious mind. I mused a little about what life had in store for the newlyweds. Later, I would wonder if what happened with our apartment was a bad omen for our friends. Their marriage was extremely short-lived. Mostly, I contemplated the future for myself. I was due at Wishard at 7 a.m. the next morning for twenty-four hours of call before the work week would begin. Then what?

I made it to the hospital on time the next morning. Thinking back, I wonder at my silliness. I told the other students on service with me and our supervising intern and resident about my misfortune, but it never occurred to me to discuss the situation with my faculty staff or perhaps even the dean of the school. Just maybe, they would have given me some time to sort things out. I just forged ahead. The only time I took off the rotation to deal with this was about thirty minutes that first day. I called my parents with the news. Late in the afternoon, I met my mom and Aunt Bonnie downstairs. They had gone shopping and bought some clothes, underwear, and toiletries for me. We traded vehicles. I put the smelly textbooks in the back of my parents' shell camper and the few items of my new wardrobe in the cab of the truck. The clothes I had gathered the night before were in the trunk of my old Pontiac, and mom and my aunt took that car home. I am sure the odor made for a less than pleasant ride. Mom washed and washed those clothes to try to salvage them. Ultimately, I think we had to throw all but two or three of my favorite college shirts away. I finished the Sunday night of call. Monday was business as usual. I left the hospital around 6 p.m. When I went out to the parking lot, still wearing the suit I had worn to a wedding two days earlier, I stood in front of that pickup, and I realized that I was homeless.

I wish I had some story about overcoming an overwhelming emotional crisis, but I really don't recall anything like that. That night, I couldn't stay anywhere around the hospital. I would have ended up on the wrong end of a news story for sure. So, I drove to the apartment complex where I lived my first year. There were relatively quiet coves in the parking lots, and I would feel safer there. I actually slept in the cab of the truck instead of back in the camper area. The small bed with its two-inch-thick mattress wasn't very appealing. Plus, the locks seemed more secure up front.

I only slept in that truck once, and I shouldn't have then. My classmates came to my rescue in force. I spent a couple nights at a time on the sofas of different people, some of whom I didn't know all that well. When I wasn't being fed by my generous benefactors, nourishment was obtained from McDonald's and vending machines. Dad sent some extra money with Mom when she came with my new supplies.

I had known my friend, Jeff Mossler, who is now a cardiologist, since we lived on the same dorm floor during our freshman year of college. He was the single occupant of his parents' house, a large home in a nice area of Indianapolis. The place was on the market, and he invited me to rent space. I had a bedroom with a twin-sized mattress on the floor, access to a bathroom, and kitchen facilities. My belongings were stored in one drawer, and the mattress was routinely placed upright in a closet. We had to keep the place looking presentable when prospective buyers came through. It was a fantastic arrangement.

I finished out the third year there with Jeff, and I have one other prominent memory of the place. Internal Medicine ended in November and those two months of surgery came next. As I was completing those surgery rotations, winter came early, and she came in earnest. I arrived at the hospital one morning a little before 5 a.m., and a light sleet was falling. The road was frozen over with a thin sheet of ice. When I tried to turn into the parking lot, I slid into the curb. There was no time to investigate the damage. I had to get my pre-rounds done before the residents arrived. When I went out that night, I saw that the rim on the right front wheel was bent. Miraculously, the tire still held air. I was able to nurse my limping car home from downtown to the northside with only a couple of people honking and pointing to let me know that my vehicle was a menace to public safety. I had traded my parents' truck back for my car long before this happened. I got my car into the garage at the Mosslers', and I knew that it would go no farther without some tender loving care. The next day was Saturday, and I bummed a ride to and from the hospital. Fortunately, we were not on call that weekend. The next day, Dad came down from Anderson with a suitable spare for long term use. He and I changed the tire in the garage. The temperature outside was twelve below zero. Inside the garage, it must have been about twelve below zero. Camp Mossy was mostly a warm experience, but there are always exceptions.

5

Electives

The fourth year of medical school was a wonderful experience. All the classes were electives, and there was very little call. The courses were located all over the place. I spent a few months in Indy, but I was able to stay at home with Mom and Dad for a couple of rotations I had in Anderson and Muncie. During one of those months, I spent time with one of the best teachers I ever had. I met Dr. Kelly Chambers when I did general Internal Medicine at Community Hospital in Anderson. In short, Dr. Chambers was the classic Rockwellian picture of a physician. He was a skilled diagnostician. He taught me to examine patients by observing them intently and really listening to them. He was kind and personable with a gentle temperament that made his patients love him. At that time, a lot of the physicians in our area were General Practitioners (GP's) who had never completed residency training, and most of them were not comfortable taking care of sicker patients in the hospital. Dr. Chambers took on the responsibility of seeing the majority of the adult inpatients, and his hospital service was very busy. He and I made morning rounds together, then he went to the office and left me at the hospital. After a few days, he had the confidence to allow me to see and start work-ups and treatment plans for the new admissions. I did not realize at the time what an honor that was. A few years later, when I was officially on staff at the hospital, I saw that Dr. Chambers did not easily relinquish the care of his patients. He served as my mentor until I left private practice. He still serves as my friend. I recently caught up with him over lunch. He is retired and spends a fair amount of his time visiting old folks at the nursing homes. "Their stories are fascinating," he said.

It was during my rotation with Dr. Chambers that I met Dr. David Bixler. It was summer, and one of the nurses was having a pool party. I was invited. The first person I saw there was Dr. Davy Jones. He was a GP, a stately gentleman, and on this occasion, he was sporting dress shoes and a Speedo. People were milling about in the usual pool party kind of way, and nobody seemed to notice Dr. Jones or the man treading water in the middle of the pool, butt naked. That was my introduction to Bix. First impression, I wasn't sure about him. In time, he would become a great friend.

Dr. Bixler was an excellent physician specializing in Intensive Care. After I became part of the staff there at Community Hospital, he and I spent many hours together, standing over patients in the ICU. We developed a respect for one another, and that evolved into a deep friendship. In contrast to Dr. Chambers, Dr. Bixler was the medical version of Elon Musk, minus all the money. Social norms were ridiculous to him. He would be seen just as often rounding on his patients at ten at night as he would at seven in the morning. I never saw him in pants other than jeans, and most of the time, he wore shorts. He frequently rode a recumbent bicycle to work. His home was a model in energy efficiency. He had solar panels and a windmill. His refrigerator was specially made with extra thick walls. If his electric bill topped ten dollars, he was pissed. One time he made a meal of grilled salmon, potatoes, and salad for a group of us who helped him replace extra heavy conversion batteries for the electrical service in his house. That was fine, except he didn't put out any silverware and started distributing the food and eating his own portion with his hands. He was an Eagle Scout and loved everything outdoors. Before I became a part of the hospital, he handcuffed himself to a tree at the edge of a wetland area to protest the hospital's plan to develop that area. He also loved the river.

Once we were canoeing down the White River. Inexperienced, I was working feverishly up front to guide our vessel. I glanced back, and there was Bix, naked as a jaybird again.

"Bix, what are you doing?"

"It's called 'canuding.'"

"Just make sure you 'canude' back there. "

In winter during my third year of private practice, Bix and his girlfriend went with my wife, Laura, and me to see "Silence of the Lambs." After the movie, he wanted to stop by the holiday party that the Emergency Department staff was holding. Shortly after we arrived, we couldn't find Bix. He showed up a little later. His hair was wet and his shoes and pants were muddy. He had been skinny dipping in the river with one of the nurses. This event was a pretty fancy little party, so he was given a lot of grief for the state of his appearance. How did he respond? He managed to engage several medical professionals in an all-out food fight.

We were an odd pair, the renegade and the rule follower. Somehow, it worked. He was a huge part of my experience at Community Hospital. In time, I would be the first to leave our little work family. Not too long after I left, he moved to Washington State. I'm not sure why, but we haven't talked much over these last few years. I still miss him. Maybe I'll give him a call. I would Facetime him, but you know the risk I'd be taking.

In addition to school-sanctioned rotations, I was able to get some valuable experience through moonlighting. During the third year, my friend and classmate, Dr. Tom Klootwyck, now the Chief Orthopedic Surgeon for the Indianapolis Colts, got me a job. He and I worked as scribes for Dr. Walker in an urgent care facility in Greenwood, IN. Because call was light in the fourth year, I was able to increase the number of shifts I worked there. I picked up two to three evening or weekend shifts each week. Our duties included seeing patients with the staff doctor, recording the encounter on the chart, writing prescriptions, and after a while, actually performing procedures such as minor laceration repairs. That would allow that attending to keep seeing patients. Although he was a crusty old guy and his wardrobe included work boots that seemed out of place for a medical care facility, working with Dr. Walker definitely enriched my education. I never heard him raise his voice to any of the staff, but they all seemed to be afraid of him. I guess his permanent scowl and very direct manner could be intimidating. I really liked the guy. He was wickedly smart. He was the most efficient physician on staff there, and he loved to teach. I watched him handle hundreds of patient encounters that included allaying fears about babies with fevers, orthopedic injuries, and starting the work-ups for more complex medical conditions. All this he did with a calm confidence that was inspiring to me.

The facility closed at 10 p.m., and one night as we were preparing to leave, a man walked in. He was ashen and sweaty. It did not take a trained medical professional to recognize that something was terribly wrong with this man. The short story is that he was having a heart attack. I was so thankful that I was working with Dr. Walker that night. He handled that emergency with the same cool efficacy that he did everything else. After the patient was tucked in the ambulance and sent on his way to the hospital, Dr. Walker reviewed with me an axiom of medical care. If you are in medicine long enough, pathology will find you, and it will usually be right before closing time.

Those three, Dr. Chambers, Dr. Bixler, and Dr. Walker were significant players in my final year of medical school. While time with them and the bulk of the fourth year passed without fireworks, there are two events that stand out in my mind. One was the result of personality, the other pathology.

After only a small amount of waffling through my early years in training, my original conviction remained sound. I was going to pursue Family Medicine. I was compelled to do a second month of surgery with Dr. Madura at University. Other than that, I tried to focus my electives on general care. I wanted to have experiences that would prepare me with a broad foundation. I spent one month on Internal Medicine with Dr. Chambers. I also arranged for a month of Family Medicine with Dr. John Salwaachter in Lebanon, IN. My plan was to spend the month leisurely seeing patients, working bankers' hours from 9 to 5, and having free time to enjoy life with my host family, the James. Dane, one of my best friends from college, was living at home with his dad and stepmom there in Lebanon, and they allowed me to stay with them. What I did not realize going in was that Dr. Salwaachter had a unique personality, and he had a little different plan in mind. He was a good physician and teacher, but his mind worked differently; it was...busy. When I worked with him, he dabbled in real estate. He had his office practice and a huge number of nursing home patients. He also served as the Medical Director of the Koala Centers for Treatment of Drug and Alcohol Addiction.

I gained some insight that I would not have received elsewhere. By that time, I had seen the results of what drugs and alcohol can do to a person, but I had not seen any formal treatment approaches. The most heartbreaking part of the experience was going to court with him for commitment proceedings. These people were being subjected to coerced treatment, and hearing the stories that led to that was heart-rending —wrecked relationships, ruined careers, lost homes, legal problems, and neglected children.

While I should have been happy and grateful that I was learning a lot, especially about addiction medicine, I was perturbed. This was the fourth year. I was not supposed to be working fourteen to sixteen hours a day. What was this maniac's problem?

Dr. Saalwachter always had me ride with him when we were working. One night about 8 p.m., we were leaving one of the nursing homes, and he said, "I need to go pick up my daughter." We were driving away from town. I didn't think much about it. "Sure, okay," I answered.

As we turned into a tiny airstrip, he said, "She's with her grandma and grandpa." Turns out he was a pilot. This was where his plane was stored. His daughter was in Illinois. Although tired and hungry, I got excited about flying in a small aircraft. I had never done that. Somewhere between take-off and our destination that excitement turned to fear. We found ourselves in the middle of a thunderstorm. Thunder and lightning boomed all around. "See if you can tell what direction it's moving," he said to me. What the hell was he talking about? As far as I could tell, it was coming from every possible direction with focused intent on destroying our tiny little airplane. Lightning crisscrossed in front, behind, over, and under us. We bounced and jolted about for what seemed like an eternity but was probably more like ten minutes. When we finally got out of that mess, I took stock of my situation—mental, physical, and spiritual. I was most relieved just to find that my pants were still clean. "We should have gone around that," he said.

"You think, you crazy bastard?!" I answered silently in my head. After all, he would be giving me a grade at the end of the rotation.

The preceptor I had for a month on a cardiology rotation at Methodist Hospital in Indianapolis was very different from Dr. Saalwachter. Dr. Martin See was about as laid back as they come. I would come to know Dr. See very well later. He switched over to the cardiology group at St. Vincent where I would do my residency. I would refer all of my heart patients to his group when I was in private practice and when I worked in the Express Care in the Emergency Department for years. Dr. See had a very dry sense of humor, and he understood the desires of a fourth-year student, little to no responsibility. I saw patients who were hospitalized, read a ton of EKG's, and watched cardiac catheterizations. The rotation was a tremendous benefit to me, and I was free from call and fourteen-hour days.

Early one Friday afternoon, Dr. See asked me to see a patient who had been admitted to the floor from the Emergency Department. When I finished her work-up, he was going to cut me loose for an early start to the weekend. The patient was an elderly lady who was well known to Dr. See. She had chronic congestive heart failure and had multiple admissions for exacerbations of that condition. She presented once again complaining of shortness of breath. Her clinical history, examination, chest x-ray, EKG, and labs were all consistent with recurrent heart failure. I wrote the note on the chart and entered typical orders. Then I tracked down Dr.See and presented her case to him. I still did complete history and physicals. As I told Dr. See about her, I said, "I don't understand. I couldn't get any reflexes at her knees." A neurological problem was not a high likelihood in the differential diagnosis, and medical students' physical examination skills are not always the most accurate.

Dr. See simply replied, "Get out of here."

When I returned on Monday morning, without preamble Dr. See walked up to me and said, "Guillain Barre. We intubated (placed a breathing tube) her about 3 o'clock Saturday morning." This lady had Guillain Barre Syndrome. It is a condition that affects the nerves. It causes ascending paralysis, that typically starts at the feet and causes weakness in the muscles as it works its way up. As in our patient's case, it can involve the nerves that control breathing, so that the patient can end up on a ventilator. Even though the absent knee reflexes was a possible tip-off, none of us felt too bad that the diagnosis had been missed on the initial assessment. First of all, Guillain Barre is rare to begin with, and this presentation was not even typical of an unusual condition.

Funny how old Dr. Walker's words rang prophetic. Pathology did find me, and it was at closing time, or at least my departure time.

6

Internship

Match Day is the day each year when medical students find out where they will be doing their residency training. We all piled back in the lecture hall where we had our first year classes. As sealed envelopes were handed out, some of my classmates were nearly apoplectic. Match is extremely stressful for many. Some fields like surgery, anesthesia, and radiology are extremely competitive. On that early spring day in 1986, I watched as people I had grown up with over the last four years, were paralyzed with fear or giddy with anticipation while waiting to open their notices. I felt none of that emotion. My first choice was the Family Medicine program at Ball Memorial Hospital in Muncie, IN. I had been assured by the administration there that I would match. When we were finally allowed to get a glimpse of our futures, I neither jumped with joy or cried in anguish as some of my colleagues did. Starting in July, I was scheduled to spend the next three years of my life at Ball

Memorial Hospital, just about twenty miles from where my parents lived. Match was anticlimactic for me.

I thought I'd chosen Ball for all the right reasons. I knew going in that I liked the residents who were already there. I liked and respected the staff. I did a rotation there my fourth year, and I was convinced that I would leave there well trained. Except for having Ball State University, Muncie was not all that different from my hometown. It felt familiar, and there was some comfort in that. I moved into an apartment, and for the first time in my life, I was living on my own. I discovered that my next door neighbor was a co-ed at Ball State, and she was cute, really cute. Things seemed to start off very well. However, the "honeymoon" ended quickly.

It was sometime in the winter when it really hit me. I hated it there. Maybe the schedule with six months of being on call every other night had something to do with it. Fatigue, more emotional than physical, might have been a factor. More likely, it was my own immaturity that played the largest role. When I woke up on the couch in my apartment and realized that I had just slept through almost half of an Indiana Hoosier basketball game, that was it. The resentment that was brewing in me started to fester into a painful boil.

Before I pulled the trigger to move from Ball, I couldn't deny that my education was enhanced by leaps and bounds. I rotated on services with different disciplines just as I had in medical school. I also had my own clinic patients whom I saw in our office two days a week. Constant exposure to patients and their problems coupled with more responsibility for their care led to higher retention and improved efficiency, and there were certainly plenty of memorable patients and cases.

Early in the year, I was placed on Obstetrics (OB). I had finished an afternoon in the office, and I was on OB call for the first time. Dr. Bob Helm, one of the senior residents, was generous with his advice and guidance. He instructed me to get up to Labor and Delivery (L&D) and make friends with all of the nurses. As the intern on call, I essentially became the Doctor of Obstetrics, for the Medicaid population of Delaware County, and Dr. Helm assured me that the Labor Room nurses could either save my butt, or not. While I had a more experienced resident on that service with me and expert faculty back-up, I knew I would often be the first point of contact for these patients. I was petrified. Obstetrics was not my strong suit. I needed any and all the help I could get. So, I did as Dr. Helm recommended. I went and chatted with the nursing staff on L&D and tried to make a good first impression.

Just as I was preparing to leave, the double doors opened abruptly. A nurse from the Emergency Department gave a cursory history as she whizzed past, pushing a young lady in a wheelchair. The history was: 23 years old, first baby, 40 plus weeks, contractions for 6 hours, feeling pressure on the perineum. The patient was leaning forward, and she was in obvious distress. She was taken straight to one of the delivery rooms. One of the nurses pulled me by the shoulder. We had a baby to deliver. The patient was undressed and given a gown. Supplies for delivery and infant resuscitation were appropriately arranged. The doctor (me!), still in street clothes, was given gloves and placed in the delivery position. We were all coaching the patient to breathe. One of the nurses used a doppler to listen over the patient's belly for the baby's heartbeat. She suddenly became quite concerned. . . she was getting nothing. I was discreetly encouraged to do a vaginal exam to determine the labor stage. I was not at all confident in my ability to accurately assess labor, but crap, this lady's cervix and uterus felt completely normal to me. When I reported this to the team, I was met with dubious expressions. One of the seasoned veterans of the nursing staff suggested with her elbow that I let her double check, and I was happy to oblige. With one of her hands on this lady's belly and the other hand with two fingers buried in the vagina, she looked as perplexed as I had been. "What is going on here?" she asked.

The patient, who had been doubling over and groaning and crying, now began to wail. It took some time, but we were finally able to determine that she was not pregnant at all. She had fabricated this elaborate tale to her friends and family. She had made up reports about visits to the obstetrician. She had morning sickness and sore breasts. She had been wearing loose clothing to hide her non-pregnant belly. She had been past her "due date" for a while. Somehow, she had to produce a baby or some other plausible end to the masquerade. She pleaded with us to tell her concerned family members, who were in the waiting area, that she had "lost the baby." After considerable counseling and encouragement, she agreed to let us bring her mom back so she could come clean with the true story. We also contacted social services to get some counseling for this girl.

Pseudocyesis, false or phantom pregnancy is extremely rare, so of course, it was my first experience in OB as a first-year resident. While I was kind to the patient and her family, honestly, I was disgusted by the ruse. I wasn't experienced and mature enough to realize how badly this girl needed help. Also looking back, I should have been grateful because that was one baby I did not have to deliver. I always felt much more at home in the ICU than I ever would in Labor and Delivery. If it came down to delivering babies or no medical career at all, I would have chosen factory work, or anything else. The program at Ball had a very strong emphasis on OB. I think that was another thing that soured my stomach there. I resented that I was being forced to spend such an inordinate amount of time and energy on something I knew I would never do in my own practice.

When I was on call for a general internal medicine service and an unattached patient was admitted to me, he or she would become my patient. I would continue to see that patient as an outpatient in our clinic. It was during one of my first of those medicine rotations that I got called to the Emergency Department to admit a patient who was reported to be in diabetic ketoacidosis (DKA). DKA is a condition that occurs in type I diabetic patients whose bodies do not make insulin. Their blood sugars go out of control and acid builds up in their bodies. It can be precipitated by infections and other medical conditions, but it is commonly caused by patients' non-compliance. On that particular day, the patient was a nineteen-year-old young man who was a student at Ball State. He was breathing on his own, but he was out of it mentally. He would respond to a painful stimulus with grunted profanities. His evaluation was consistent with profound DKA. That was how I met Michael.

Usually DKA patients are gratifying for physicians and staff to care for because the condition tends to respond, often dramatically, to treatment. We admitted Michael to the ICU very early in the morning. When I made it back to check on him in the afternoon, he was fully awake and alert. The nursing staff was already growing weary of him in those few, short hours. He was requesting, well actually demanding, a lot of service. I was able to learn more about him. He had been diagnosed with diabetes at age six. He had been treated for DKA many times. He knew the routine. He also had an intellectual understanding of the ongoing, long-term management of his condition. One thing had not changed from the early morning hours. He still had an admirable command of the use of profanity. He had been in a lot of hospitals, "a hell of a lot better than this f@#(*&^ s*%$ hole."

I would be involved about six more times that year when Michael would be admitted either with sky-high or rock bottom blood sugars. It quickly became clear that his understanding of diabetes and the rationale for treatment was not translating into his life. I saw him in my office. I asked psychiatry to see him repeatedly, and it seemed like the only thing we ever got out of that was that he was "not psychotic." We got information from boys who lived on his dorm floor. He was a binge drinker. They also witnessed him do things like eat a pound bag of M&M's and then theatrically draw up a syringe full of insulin to inject himself to cover the dietary indiscretion.

We had a multidisciplinary meeting with Michael, his parents, social services, administration, and psychiatry. After that meeting, his mother and I lingered in the hallway outside the conference room. She was glad that I had spoken up pretty strongly that, psychotic or not, unless things changed dramatically and soon, he was going to kill himself. Dealing with Michael's outrageous histrionics was impossible, but trying to get someone else besides his mother and me to see the flashing red warning signs was even worse.

Including my experiences with Michael, my education and experience exploded there at Ball, but I just wasn't happy. I was restless. I started looking for something different. I had friends in the Family Medicine program at St. Vincent (St.V) Hospital in Indianapolis. They let me know there was an opening for a second-year position. I jumped at the opportunity. The staff at Ball was none too happy with me for abandoning ship. The only ambivalence I had about leaving was that I had a sense of loyalty to those who had taught me. However, the bitterness I felt toward the institution for trying to work me to death won out in the end. One day in May, as college students were packing up to leave for the summer, I finally met back up with my neighbor in our parking lot. She looked confused as she said, "I thought you moved out months ago." Of course she would have thought that; I was always at the stupid hospital. As I drove out of Muncie with my car fully loaded, heading for greener pastures at St.V, I stopped my car in front of Ball Memorial Hospital. I gave them a "salute" that spoke more of my sophomoric demeanor than of any mistreatment I received there.

The transition to life at St. Vincent was great. I was back living with my old pal, Mark Kemper. He and his wife had a big house with extra space that they graciously let me occupy. I reconnected with friends from medical school who were in the program. I made an instant connection with Dr. Dave Johnson who was a year behind me in training. He and I seemed to always be placed on the same rotations together. My first rotation was on Cardiology, the trump card for which St. Vincent was known, and my preceptor on that service, Dr. Hallam, was fantastic.

I had been at St. Vincent for about eight weeks when the secretary in our office told me that I had a phone call. I knew a patient would not have been patched through directly. I was curious as I picked up the line. It was Michael's mom. She was calling to tell me that our worry had been well-founded, and she thanked me for everything I had tried to do for her son. Michael was dead. His body had been discovered in his apartment that morning. All these years later, I can still remember the tone of that conversation. It wasn't sadness or anger. There was an expression of dead, hollow defeat in that monotone voice on the other end of that phone call. It was only after becoming a father myself, a few years later, that I began to understand that the voice of my patient's mother expressed an impenetrable void that would forever be in her heart. At a time when things seemed to be going great for me, I was learning that the world has its own way of mixing bad with the good.

7

Residency

Just before I left Ball, Dr. Bock, a psychologist who worked with residents, took me aside for a chat. He told me that he had worked with a student named Laura, in the nursing program a couple years earlier, and he was sure that she was working at St.Vincent. He thought she and I would get along well. He wrote her name down for me and suggested that I look her up. I thanked him, but had no intention of following through with his recommendation. Who does anything with that kind of advice? I wish I had saved that piece of paper he gave me instead of tossing it in the trash as soon as he was out of sight. Two years later that girl he was talking about became my wife.

I think it was the second day of my first rotation at St.V that Dr. Hallam and I went to see a patient in the Cardiac Recovery area. It was early morning. There was a nurse sitting up on one of the low countertops. She had on a scrub dress that showed off great legs. When I saw her name tag, I said, "Hey, Dr. Bock told me I should look you up here."

She was tired from working all night, but her smile brightened a little. She said, "He sent me a note, too." We went out shortly after that and have been together ever since.

Call was not nearly as frequent for me as it had been the year before. Maybe because I wanted to spend as much time as I could with Laura, but mostly because I was a childish dolt, I still did not relish being on call. I always did the work and turned on compassion and even charm for the patients and their families. I would just complain to anyone and everyone else while doing it. One evening as call was just beginning, I was getting the chart for my new admission, and I was grumbling to a fellow resident about our terrible plight. Dr. William Nasser, a renowned pioneer in cardiology who was recognized worldwide, happened to be working in the same workstation. I had never met him, but I certainly knew who he was. He couldn't help overhearing my expressions of displeasure. He stopped what he was doing. He came and guided me gently by the elbow off to the side. There, without any introduction, he explained to me what a great learning experience call could be. He said I should embrace the opportunity and appreciate the honor. He did not wait for a response. He didn't need one. He simply returned to his work and left me to ponder. My attitude did not completely change overnight, but when someone of Dr. Nasser's stature goes out of his way to teach you like that, you pay attention. I would refer patients to Dr. Nasser and his group when I got out into private practice. Years later, when I was the President of the Medical Staff at Community Hospital in Anderson, I was able to help Dr. Nasser with a problem he was having getting credentialing for some of his partners expedited. My little favor paled in comparison to the gift he had given me that evening.

Just as at Ball, there were plenty of memorable patients at St.V. I first met Wilma, when she presented to the office with a god-awful rash on one side of her face. She had shingles. That problem resolved without any long-term effects. Wilma was a taciturn little lady whose wig was always slightly askew. Her thrift store dresses seemed to swallow her small frame, and she wore stockings that wrinkled at the ankles. At first, I struggled to get information from her. In time, without wasting a lot of words, she would express herself very directly, and she would openly challenge me if she thought I was going down the wrong path with her medical care. I thought she was great. We fell into routine office care of a fairly common set of problems for an elderly woman: high blood pressure, arthritis, poor eyesight, and congestive heart failure (CHF).

Not obvious initially, it would become apparent that Wilma had a desire for more personal information about her doctor. Her often-abrupt mode of inquiry left me with no choice but to respond. Honestly, I didn't mind sharing with her. We became friends. She found out I was engaged to Laura. She learned of my southern heritage, and that gave us a stronger bond. She was a transplanted southerner from Mississippi. In the middle of our office assessment one day, she blurted out, "I bet you like beans."

"Sure do," I replied.

"I make the best beans," she said.

An invitation was extended and accepted. Laura and I went to Wilma's for beans and cornbread. Wilma had a caretaker who did not live with her, but stayed late one evening to help her prepare dinner for her doctor. Torrential rains had soaked the city earlier in the day, and we found the parking lot at Wilma's apartment complex to be flooded. I carried Laura as I trudged through a giant puddle to get to the stairway that led up to her apartment. Wilma was so proud that we came to her home for a southern supper. Everything looked and smelled wonderful. As Laura and I each took our first bites, we glanced at one another...salty! With a couple of refills of water, we made it through the meal and made over our hostess with overflowing praise and gratitude. She was beaming as we left. I don't often hear of doctors and patients having close friendships where they would dine together today. I think the shuffling and trading of physicians and patients among insurance plans and health systems, like they are cards in some giant board game, has something to do with that. Many times they are just starting to get to know one another when they move on to a new policy or practice group.

If I had been astute as a clinician, alarm bells would have sounded loudly in my head, but I missed it. Too much salt can cause a person with congestive heart failure to crash, and that is exactly what happened. That dinner was on Wednesday. Two days later I was on Family Medicine call when Wilma was admitted through the Emergency Department in respiratory distress caused by an exacerbation of her CHF. I intubated her and put her on a ventilator in the ICU. I wasn't on call the rest of the weekend, but because I was her doctor and I felt like I was to blame for her current condition, I managed her care myself. With the help of the nursing staff in the ICU, I was able to get her stabilized over the weekend, and we weaned her off the ventilator early Monday morning. When I checked back on her at lunch time, she was doing great. She was complaining about how bland the food was. I made damn sure she was not eating salt while she was in the hospital.

Even though I wrote orders to have her moved out of the ICU, I was informed that I had to have a Critical Care consult. Dr. Ron Resiman was the head of the ICU. I had gotten to know him when I was on a Pulmonary rotation with Dr. Steve McAdams, who managed a lot of the ventilator patients. I caught up with Dr. Reisman and asked if he would consult for me. I gave him a two minute history. Already busy and overworked, he begrudgingly agreed. I stood at the bedside as he did his consultation. He waved at Wilma and wrote in the chart, "As managed by Dr. Smith." He nodded toward me, handed me the chart, and in typical Reisman fashion, he roared off like a buzzsaw. It was one of the greatest compliments I ever received during my training.

Wilma was discharged a day or so later. Until I finished residency, I continued to see her regularly in the office. She was the only patient Laura and I invited to our wedding. We had to provide transportation for her. My friend, Chris Bratton, graciously agreed to pick her up. He still occasionally tells the story about their time together. He stopped for gas, and being the kind of person he is, he asked if she wanted anything. She said she wanted some gum. When he returned to the car and handed her a couple packs of gum she said, "Is that all they had?" Laura and I were married in March. I probably saw Wilma two or three more times before I left at the end of June. I should have kept in touch, but I never heard from or of her again.

In addition to developing relationships with patients like Wilma, I got established in nice, comfortable working collaboration with other residents and students. It felt good that I was consulted regularly by younger peers. I also got great feedback from supervising staff like Dr. Hallam and Dr. Reisman. Most seemed to think I might have something to contribute to the medical profession, but not all.

While on Pediatrics, we rotated through the Neonatal Intensive Care Unit (NICU), the place where sick newborns, especially premature babies are cared for. Through our training in Family Medicine, we got a lot of exposure and experience with pediatric patients. Most of us became proficient with procedures common in that discipline, including lumbar punctures (LP), more commonly known as spinal taps. Believe it or not, that procedure is easier to perform on a baby than it is on an adult. Late one afternoon, one of the staff neonatologists was being pulled in a hundred different directions. She was attending to the needs of some very sick newborns. She needed to do a follow-up LP on a baby who had been in the NICU for a while. I volunteered to stay to do it for her.

A nurse positioned the baby so she was lying on her side with knees and forearms pushed together. She became a little ball, and her back presented a rounded target. I prepared the skin with sterilizing soap and placed a drape as I had done many times. Just as I started to put the needle through the skin the baby squirmed and the nurse's hand slipped. The tip of the needle barely nicked the skin well away from the intended landmark. I dabbed one time with a gauze and the minimal bleeding stopped. We simply redressed everything, and with a new spinal needle the procedure was easily completed. Specimens were labeled and sent to the lab. I said so long to the staff neonatologist, and went on my way, thinking I had done a good deed.

The next day, we made rounds with a different neonatologist. When we got to the patient I had performed the LP on the previous afternoon, she made an elaborate production of pulling down the baby's diaper. "Who did this?" she asked, as she pointed to a tiny scab that had formed over the nick in the skin. I spoke up immediately and tried to explain what happened. She cut me off. She made it clear that if someone didn't know what he was doing, he wouldn't work without direct supervision on any of the babies. In fact, any procedures done by any of us (residents) for the rest of the rotation, had to be done with an attending standing over us.

That wasn't the end of it. She rode my ass relentlessly for the rest of the rotation. If I answered any question posed on rounds, she pointed out how egregiously incorrect I was. If you believe that only a small percentage of communication is delivered in the words spoken, then I think you would have agreed that this staff doctor's facial expressions and body language suggested I was an incompetent boob who had no place in medicine. You might think I am exaggerating, but my fellow trainees appreciated the situation for what it was too. Dr. Paul Hamori was an Internal Medicine resident. IM people didn't spend a lot of time with pediatric training. I'm not sure if that rotation was required or elective for him. I just remember that he was there, and one day as we left the NICU, he put his arm around my shoulders and said, "Doug, I am so sorry for you."

This doctor was already a respected neonatologist when this happened. After that, she continued to do fantastic work caring for sick infants. She held leadership roles and administrative duties in medical education, and she was good at them. I don't know why she reacted the way she did. Maybe a parent or nurse complained about seeing that little nick, and that caused more stress for her. Maybe she truly thought I was an idiot. I just know I was glad that incident happened toward the end of the rotation, and I was extremely thankful for the support from Dr. Hamori. Small gestures really do mean a lot.

All of that transpired in the hospital, but most of the third year shifted emphasis toward office and outpatient care. There was very little call. It provided time for reading, studying, and preparing for the next stage of life. From late fall, early winter 1988, I started looking to find a practice location. Dr. Walker called and offered me a job in his Urgent Care, but I had my heart set on a traditional Family Practice. His practice was Urgent Care, and it was on the southside of Indy. That was too far from home. Laura and I were moving to Anderson.

8

Private Practice –
The Early Years

Out of residency, I got hired to join Dr. Bill VanNess in his practice in the small town of Summitville, IN. Laura and I moved to Anderson as planned. Laura's dad was a realtor, and he helped us close on our first home. The commute to the office was about fifteen miles. The hospital where we would send our inpatients was Community Hospital in Anderson. It was a little west of midway between our house and the office. The logistics seemed great. Bill was a good clinician, and he was very interested in the politics of medicine. Partly because he had the outside activity in the state medical association, he was busier than he wanted to be. That's why he took on a partner. It took awhile for me to figure out that there was too much work there for one provider, but really not enough for two. I left that practice after almost two years to open my own shop right across the street from the hospital, but before I exited that brief and long chapter in that old office building attached to the tiny Summit Convalescent Center, I received an indoctrination into life in real-world medicine that would accurately represent what I would come to feel about my entire career in clinical medicine and life. When I received that phone call at St. V informing me that my former patient had died, I started to realize that no stage of life is all good or all bad. My experiences in Summitville reinforced that idea.

Summitville was a tiny farming community. It also had a small pallet factory. The people there were salt of the earth, no bullshit kind of people. They spoiled me with their direct, no exaggeration explanations of their symptoms and problems. They genuinely wanted to get well so they could get back to work. Years later, when I was working the second coverage position in the Emergency Department at St.Vincent Hospital, which drew from some of the more affluent communities outside of Indianapolis, I often found many of the patients to be entitled. I would find myself longing for my straight forward farm folk.

Sometimes those endearing personality traits could lead to some interesting situations. Frugal by necessity, most of the farming patients expected to pay for our services, but they expected value at a fair price. One of my earliest patients there was a gentleman about sixty-five years old. He was a prototype Summitville farmer, congenial but direct. His skin was weathered from years of exposure, and he was a little round in the middle. The rugged work in the fields and livestock yards was typically no match for the midwestern appetite for good home cooking. He presented with a description of recurring chest pain that was not textbook but was somewhat worrisome for a heart problem. Since heart disease is the leading killer in our country, I was not taking any chances with this man. At his first visit, we completed an EKG and sent him for a chest x-ray and a treadmill heart test. He returned a week later, and we reviewed that his tests were normal. He was still having the pain, and it was really bothering him. At that visit, the description sounded more like muscular pain likely due to a chest wall strain. I prescribed some local treatment and a generic muscle relaxer. About a week later, he showed up at the office unannounced, and he was angry. Nikki was the person in our office who greeted patients as they checked in. She was both sweet and street-wise tough. Even she was surprised by the aggression this guy displayed. He explained that he was not any better. He slammed the pill bottle containing the muscle relaxers I had prescribed down on the counter, and the tablets sprayed all over Nikki's face and chest. He made it clear that he was "not about to finance Dr. Smith's jet plane," and, "What about this damn rash?"

Ding, ding, ding. Before shingles breaks out in a rash it will often cause pain for many days. Sometimes the pain is more typical of nerve irritation pain that implies shingles, but often, as with this man, it is vague, hard to describe, and not recognizable.

The commotion got all of us in the office up front in a hurry. We quickly ushered the farmer into a room for two reasons. One was to quell the disturbance. He was upsetting everybody in the building, including the other patients. The other was for his personal protection. He had crossed two lines with Nikki. She also grew up in a culture of honor that instilled in her that she shouldn't take any shit, and she would protect herself if she felt threatened. It turned out she would protect an employer, too, if she really liked him. She was as loyal as the day is long. She stayed with me until I left private practice altogether, and she ran interference for me many more times. While the rest of my staff calmed her down, I dealt with the patient.

It took some direct, honest discussion, but I was able to appease him and prescribe a new treatment plan. He was satisfied and contrite as he left. He continued to be our patient there until I left to open my own practice. From that point on, I always tried to remember to tell patients whose pain we couldn't explain to call if they developed a rash.

I found the clientele in Summitville to be gritty. Generally, it was the men who did the rugged farm work, but their wives and daughters were just as tough. One day, a demure, elderly lady, with tired blue eyes and white hair pulled back in a tight bun, was brought in by her daughter. She looked down or away from me, and her daughter did the talking. The complaint was that "mom stinks." She had not been to a doctor for many years. I tried to put her at ease by talking softly and explaining that I would just like to check her over a little. I let her know what each move would be. She was dressed in a loose-fitting, cotton summer dress. She did not want to change into an examination gown. I asked if I could remove some tissues that were poking out from under the top of the dress on the left. They were actually sticking out of her bra on the left side. I needed to move them to get a good listen to her heart. She neither agreed nor disagreed, so, I proceeded cautiously. I found the source of mom's stench. Underneath those tissues was a huge, fungating mass that clearly originated from the breast. When I asked how long she had dealt with that, she replied, "A while." I asked about pain, and she said her right side and left leg "hurt a little." Her liver, lungs, and bones were riddled with the disease. Too tough for her own good, she died of breast cancer a few weeks later.

In addition to being frugal and tough, these small-town people also had a fun-loving side that I really enjoyed. They could joke in a way that demonstrated a childlike mischief that fit my sense of humor, and they rarely crossed that thin line of good taste. The office was located in an old, but warm and inviting building that was connected to the smallest nursing home I have ever seen. It was home to about twenty patients. I think Bill had eighteen of them, and I had two. One day at lunch, I was going back to check on one of my patients. There was a narrow hallway that led from a common living area to the nurses' workstation and the actual patient rooms. I was walking behind one of the nurses who worked there. She was absolutely, magazine quality, gorgeous. She was tall, dark, and shapely. She had a bright smile, and she had a sweet personality that made her even more beautiful. As we were walking, one of the residents there, a retired farmer who had been diminished by the relentless ravages of age, was approaching us from the opposite direction. He was able to propel himself by stepping while seated in a wheelchair that had the footrests removed. When the nurse drew even with him, he reached out and grabbed her firmly on the rear end. Instantly, she bent down, and directly face-to-face gave him a fifteen-second verbal barrage that would have sent me reeling. He didn't flinch. Furious, she stomped off down the hall. Shocked and amused by the entire scene, I honestly did not even know what to think. When I got to the old guy, I hesitated briefly, and he gave me the biggest, most exaggerated wink that I think was supposed to be conspiratorial. I guess you can forgive an old geezer one transgression across the threshold of moral decency. I know my nurse friend eventually did.

Each person on the medical staff at the hospital was required periodically to take call for the hospital. While on call, he or she would be responsible for the care of unattached patients who were admitted to the hospital. Like Michael at Ball, I met Dolly when she was admitted in a state of diabetic ketoacidosis. Dolly was in her mid-forties, and she was infamous. I think she had been an inpatient seventeen times the year before I inherited her. She was short, very round, and toothless. Her mostly gray hair was thin and stringy. She had dirt under her fingernails, and she had scars on her arms where she constantly scratched. She would be my patient for about five years before she ended up on dialysis and living in a nursing home. Caring for Dolly was extremely challenging, but it was always entertaining. She had a quick wit and grit that gave her a certain appeal. Despite living in familial dysfunction that included raising two fatherless children in extreme poverty, she could generally find something to laugh about, and her complaints about her plight were frequently humorous. I got a kick out of her.

Like most of the patients I acquired while in Summitville, she would follow me when I moved to my new office in Anderson. At both places, when she would enter the reception area, she looked assiduously for reactions to her presence. If another patient or family member in the waiting room showed the slightest visible repulsion to her physical appearance, she was sure to take a seat as close to that person as possible, and most often, she would strike up a conversation.

One day near the end of our time in Summitville, she was in the office. As I was writing her prescriptions, I was confused about the strength of the nitroglycerin patch she was wearing after a recent admission to the hospital. I went back into the exam room. Thinking she could just remind me, I left the door ajar, and asked, "Dolly, what size is your nitro patch?" Before I realized what was happening, Dolly lifted the tent-like muumuu she was wearing straight up over her head. Her intent was for me to look at the patch. Just at that moment, one of our nurses was leading another patient back to the lab draw area. The three of us were briefly exposed to Dolly in all of her glory.

Shortly after we opened up shop in Anderson, Dolly stormed into the office without an appointment. She was crying and yelling. The staff took her straight back to our pro-

cedure room, and pulled me out of one of the other examination rooms. After several minutes, we were finally able to
make out that her distress was caused by a problem with one
of her ears. With much coaxing and calming, I was able to get
a peek, and just a minute later, I was able to extract the cock-
roach that had burrowed deep inside her ear canal. Almost in
an instant, Dolly was back to her usual self. She planned to
capture as many of the vermin as she could and stuff them
under the door to her complex manager's apartment. She
hoped a roach would crawl up his butt. (paraphrased)

Even with her progressively failing kidneys, in the last year
I was her doctor, she was admitted to the hospital only four
times. We considered that a major victory. When she went on
dialysis, she didn't have the resources to get back and forth
to the treatment center and just generally care for herself. I
didn't see patients in the nursing home where she ended up,
but I did go to visit her once. "Dolly-do-dunkaroo," I said as
I walked in her room.

"What the hell are you doing here?" was her reply. There
was no doubt in my mind that she was glad that I came. I
was, too.

Before I landed in Anderson with Dolly in tow, I was
beginning to realize that the trip to and from Summitville
had not been without its problems. One time, I messed up.
I misread my schedule. I made morning rounds in Anderson
and drove to Summitville, only to receive a page from the
hospital. I had a patient waiting for me to do her sigmoidoscopy. Sigmoidoscopy is a procedure used to look at the anus,

rectum, and sigmoid colon with a lighted scope. I was trained to do them during my residency, and I wanted to do some procedures in my practice. Disregarding every traffic law ever written, I drove back to the hospital, fifteen miles away in Anderson, did the exam, and flew back to the office. I was over an hour behind when I finally started seeing patients, and that only grew as the day progressed. The patients were frustrated, and the staff was just plain ol' pissed.

Another time, it was late in the afternoon. I kept getting calls from a nurse on one of the medicine wards at the hospital. A patient I had admitted there was steadily getting worse, and the adjustments that I was making to her care over the phone were not helping. Finally, I had one more patient to see. Before I went in with that patient, I got a report from the nurse again. Things were deteriorating quickly. I asked for the patient to be transferred to the ICU. I called the ICU and asked the nurse to have set-ups for an arterial line and a triple lumen central venous catheter ready for me. All that is just doctor-speak for the patient was really sick and needed a lot of care. The last office patient was dispatched, and I scrambled out of the office. I was barreling south toward the hospital when the red and blue lights came on behind me. I pulled over. As the sheriff's deputy approached the car, I rolled down the window, stuck my head out, and naively said "I am a doctor, and I am on my way to Community to see a patient I just transferred to the ICU."

He took a step back, placed both hands on his hips, and replied, "Is that so?" Yes sir, he was in charge. He detained me there for over twenty minutes and gave me a ticket. Raging, I stormed into the ICU and vented to all who cared to listen. Through a quick ad hoc meeting of ICU nursing personnel, support staff, and myself, a decision was made. I was not going to pay that damn ticket.

My parents were indignant and had to get involved. They called the Madison County Sheriff's office and got nowhere. I ended up consulting with a lawyer who happened to be a partner of the judge who would be overseeing my case in Edgewood City Court. I guess the officer involved gets to choose the venue to make it as convenient as he can for himself. My lawyer said I should represent myself, and he was sure the judge would "take it under advisement." If anyone ever wanted to make a documentary about a fish out of water, he should have just filmed me in that dang courtroom. I was, and fortunately still am, not very familiar with courtroom proceedings. I brought copies of medical records showing that I was indeed at the hospital immediately after being stopped. The judge, not the prosecuting attorney, questioned the authenticity of those documents. Strike one. That the doctor was being whittled to a frazzle seemed to gain the interest of all the other people in court that day. I saw the looks of amusement all around as the prosecutor expertly performed his job and quickly demonstrated that the deputy had used a radar gun that had been calibrated for correct functioning earlier in the day, and using that reliable instrument the deputy had clocked me at 15 mph over the speed limit. Strike two. The prosecutor, Packy Cunningham, was sort of a friend. I knew his kids, and one of my best friends was dating one of his daughters at the time. I think because he wanted to relieve some of my obvious anxiety, he asked at the end if the patient had done well. Having lost all of my bravado, I simply answered, "She did." As I drove home, I beat myself for not providing more entertainment for the throng that had watched me squirm. I wished I had answered Packy with, "She did, but it was no thanks to that jack-wagon," referring to the deputy who sat smugly with a smirk on his face throughout the entire ordeal. It was probably best that for once I kept my foot out of my mouth.

The judge had, just as my lawyer had predicted, finally said, "Ok, I'm going to consider this matter under advisement. You'll be notified of my judgment in the mail." Really? I hadn't completely struck out? It took several weeks before two things related to that hearing occurred at almost the same time. I received a notice in the mail. My fine was reduced to something like ten dollars, but I had to pay court costs. In all, it was financially more expensive than it would have been if I had just paid the fine. Not a complete strikeout, but not a hit either. Maybe one or two days after getting the verdict, I was back at the hospital one evening after the office had closed. I turned the corner onto one of the wards where I had admitted a patient earlier in the day. There, leaning against the counter, talking with the Unit Secretary, was that damn deputy who had given me the ticket. That pecker worked part-time security at my hospital!

I would not miss that commute.

9

Private Practice – Anderson

Because there was no other office space available, the hospital pushed forward a renovation project they had planned for the future. A small house that sat directly in front of the hospital on the opposite side of Madison Avenue became my very own doctor's office. My shingle was out in my hometown, and it did not take long before the waiting area, three exam rooms, and the procedure room in that quaint little building were filled with patients. Quite a few of those patients were older adults who had watched me grow up. Many shared a similar attitude. They were there to support a boy who had "done good."

I fell into a routine fairly quickly. I would make rounds at the hospital in the morning before the office opened. We would see patients in the office from 8 a.m. to 5 p.m., except for Thursday when we knocked off at noon. After the office closed, I would go back to the hospital to tie up loose ends. I also had patients in three nursing homes. It was hard for me to work in a convenient time for the required visits for those patients. I seemed to always be writing on their charts while Jeopardy!, apparently a favorite of the "wizened generation," was playing on televisions in the various common rooms. Since I was an early rounder, getting to the hospital between five and six-thirty in the morning, and Jeopardy! aired at seven-thirty at night, that meant my workdays were generally ten to fourteen hours long. At first, I saw that necessary time commitment as a badge of honor, but time and fatigue, brutal physical, mental, and emotional fatigue, has a way of changing a person's perspective.

On top of feeling exhausted most of the time, I was terrible at running a business. Once when insurance payments were lagging behind, Laura and I had to take money back out of our very modest bank account to make payroll for the staff. Going in, I just thought I could out-work any obstacles and money would take care of itself. For four years, I ran my own show. That included sixty to eighty-hour work weeks and bringing home the same amount of money my dad was drawing from his GM pension. Eventually, I was left with only enough energy to be a pain in the ass grouch.

If my conversations were not about IU basketball, and at that point, we had not won a championship in almost a decade, they were all dominated by my constant complaining. Add a few beers and the ferocity of that grumbling went to a whole new level. Looking back, I don't know how my friends and family could stand to be around me.

The strain of my discontent was no more apparent than in my marriage. Laura tried her best to support me, but the rage that constantly simmered just beneath the surface frequently found expression. She was usually not the intended target; she just frequently walked into the line of fire. Stupidly, we made things worse. In an attempt to make finances work, she came to work in the office. A couple of things made that a bad idea. It did not improve our bottom line, and she was exposed to my rants nearly twenty-four seven. In the back office where I dictated charts, my nurses would get to share in my displeasure about whatever dipwad-patient, administrator, insurance company, consultant was deliberately making my life miserable on any given day. I would go on to do my evening rounds after the office. Unless something ticked me off on the way, I usually would not want to discuss the office or hospital when I got home. However, if I had crossed a line earlier in the day and made it seem that Laura or any of our other staff was the dipwad of the hour, Laura would want to discuss it, and she had learned to discuss things well. She had learned to fight.

I'm afraid, during that stage of our relationship, I was rubbing off on her more than the other way around. In addition to developing an aggressive side, she began to concede to a notion that was already in full bloom in my mind. There was something that was never mentioned in her nurses' training, and I don't remember ever hearing anything about it while I was in medical school: *patients were inconveniencing our lives.*

One time, we were getting ready to leave the office for the day. She happened to glance out the window. "Oh God, someone's puking out there." Obviously displeased, she still went dutifully to help the poor slob who was retching in our parking lot. It was my brother. He was having his first migraine headache, and he looked like death warmed over. A possible alternative diagnosis to a migraine like his was a brain hemorrhage. I took him across the street to the hospital and arranged for a neurologist to see him. He got a head CT and a spinal tap. His work-up was negative, and he responded to treatment for migraine. That interruption made me even later than usual getting home. "Is T. OK?" she asked as soon as I walked in. I said that he was. Clearly she was relieved, but she couldn't completely hide a tiny element of resentment — another evening given to, no, taken by medicine.

Even while I was dragging along disgruntled and bitter, medicine had a way of providing some incredible moments. I can't imagine that I will ever forget some of the things that I experienced. It was a spring afternoon when one of our elderly patients came to the office. She was painfully thin and frail. Years of smoking had permanently stained the tips of her fingers brown, wrinkled her skin, and lowered her voice to a whisper that was barely audible. She was hunched forward so that her lower ribs almost met her hip bones. That day she was not forthcoming with the reason for her visit. I finally realized that she was embarrassed about something, and I was able to put her at ease enough for her to tell us that she had a vaginal discharge. She had a condition called uterine prolapse where her cervix and uterus would literally protrude out of her vagina. Years before I inherited her as a patient, she had been given a pessary, which is like a hard diaphragm that fits in the vagina to hold the uterus in place. Women usually insert and remove that device themselves, and they are taught to take it out and clean it at least every three months. Most women do it a lot more frequently than that. She wasn't sure exactly when, but she knew hers had not been removed in over two years. With a lot of help and support from Jennifer, one of the nurses in our office, we managed to do her pelvic exam and extract this firm plastic disc that was covered in putrid green slime. As repulsive as the visual appearance of that thing was, it was nothing compared to the odor. We were greeted with the most noxious smell ever imagined. Jennifer and I were gagging, and our poor little patient was mortified. More than twenty-five years later, the thought of that stench still makes me snurl my nose and feel just a little nauseated. We closed off that room for the rest of that day and the next day, and had box fans blowing exhaust out open windows. After a day and a half of ventilation and a couple of cans of orange-scented air freshener, we were able to use that room again. As disgusting as it was for everyone involved, it was extremely gratifying for me. Just like pulling the bug out of Dolly's ear, simply removing the foreign body and having this patient engage in some regular hygiene fixed her problem. As far as I know, she never had any more issues with her pessary. She died a few years later due to her chronic lung disease.

There were plenty of other interesting encounters, and I had a sense of loyalty to my patients. However, in the end, that lifestyle was simply not sustainable. I was going crazy, and Laura was getting fed up with me. Something had to give, and I believe fate intervened. One night, I was talking with my friend from residency, Dr. Dave Johnson. Straight out of training, he started working in the Express Care in the Emergency Department at St.Vincent, and they had an opening. "Are you serious about wanting to get out of private practice?" he asked me.

"I'm dead serious. I absolutely cannot do this anymore," I answered without any hesitation.

Yes, I was tired of the long hours, and barely eking out a living. I was absolutely fed up with being on call. I gave my fourteen hours, and then there was always some numb-skull who wanted something more from me. I wanted to be left the hell alone sometimes. All of that was true, but there was something much more that was nagging me deep inside where I was afraid to look. I said previously that I wanted to be a very good doctor. That didn't express my true ambition. I wanted to be "the best." I wanted to be perfect.

In that environment, I was struggling every day to keep up. Sometimes when I ran an EKG in the office on a patient, worrying that my interpretation wasn't one hundred percent correct, I would ruminate over it for days. I rehashed and deliberated over treatment plans for hours. I carried charts home with me at night because the documentation had to be exactly precise. The reason I made rounds so early in the morning was that it took me longer than my colleagues to see patients. The nurses loved working with me, and I got a reputation for being "thorough." Like those who labeled me "determined" when I was a student, they had no idea there was something brewing, unseen and unheard. They didn't know that when they had to call me because I had forgotten something or if they just needed to clarify an order, it gutted me. That meant I had failed. I had made a mistake. Not only did I see that I was occasionally making those miscues, but I had some blunders that were much more serious. Once I prescribed amoxicillin for a patient and friend whose chart had a big red sticker on it — Allergy: penicillin. I misdiagnosed an infant who had pyloric stenosis (a condition that causes the stomach to not empty) with reflux. I was making some bad mistakes.

Nurses were misinterpreting orders. Patients couldn't give a straight history, and they wouldn't follow instructions. How the hell were they supposed to get any better when they wouldn't do what I told them? My staff wasn't paying attention. "They" were causing me to screw up. I knew that, somehow, someway, somebody was going to get my ass sued. It was impossible for anybody to be an exceptional doctor in that setting. There had to be something better. My answer to Dr. Johnson that night could not have been more correct. I couldn't do it anymore. (Is it possible that I had set ridiculous, unrealistic, detrimental standards for myself? Nah, it had to be the situation.)

Dr. Johnson arranged for me to meet with the managing partners at St. Vincent Emergency Physicians (SVEP) a few days later. He already told me what the practice was like. Really, the meeting was about me selling myself. Apparently, I did all right, because after about twenty minutes, I shook hands with Dr. Steve Jardina and Dr. Stewart Bick, and the deal was done. I was closing my practice. The next day, I made the announcement and started making the necessary arrangements to shut the office down completely. Six weeks later, the doors were figuratively shuttered, and about a week and a half after that, I walked into the Express Care for the first shift in my new career in Urgent Care/Emergency Medicine.

The drive from the parking lot at St. Vincent to our house in Moonsville, IN, where we lived at the time, took about an hour and ten minutes. That night while driving home, after I left Dr. Jardina and Dr. Bick, I answered five calls from the answering service and hospital. With my new position, there would be no after hours call. There would definitely be some things that I was not going to miss about private practice.

10

"Sorty" a Doctor

Without question, those closest to me would have rubber stamped me as a dissatisfied malcontent for most of the time I was in practice in Anderson. I also think I hid it pretty well from most outsiders. At least, there was a huge expression of shock and dismay from colleagues, administrators, patients, nurses, pharmaceutical reps, and acquaintances when I decided to leave private practice. Maybe I was still able to treat people right despite being miserable on the inside. Also, there definitely were many happy moments mixed in with the relentless grind I have described. I had family who loved and supported me, and they provided most of the cheerful times. One of the more entertaining family experiences was when my grandpa came to Indiana to visit.

Grandpa outlived Granny by many years. He did everything wrong to be able to enjoy longevity, but somehow he beat the odds. He lived to be ninety-eight, and he was very active until he was ninety-two. He smoked, chewed tobacco, poured bacon grease over his food, and drank a little whiskey every day. He was tall and strong, and he believed in hard work. He was a concrete mason by trade, and he was always involved in some kind of farming. My earliest memory of him was watching as he planted corn using mules and a plow. At his funeral, the preacher recalled a story in which it had been said that when it was too hot to work the mules, my grandpa might have been seen clearing a fence row by hand.

He was also cross-eyed. I never knew if he was looking at me. I inherited that disorder. I was a cross-eyed kid. My parents consulted an ophthalmologist for my condition, and he recommended surgery. My grandfather disagreed vehemently with Mom and Dad when they decided to proceed with the operation. That is the only time I ever knew of Arlie Jackson Smith not getting his way. Thank God my parents didn't give in to his bullying. My surgery was a success. The only residual effect I have is the inability to look through anything that is binocular.

Early in my last year of college, Dad and I stopped overnight at Granny and Pa's. We were on our way to East Tennessee State for my interview at their medical school. Grandpa could not get his head around what might cause me to look at schools outside of Indiana. Despite reassurances ad nauseum, he became convinced that I was circumventing some sort of trouble. As we were getting in the car to leave, he was still asking my dad what kind of mess I had gotten myself into.

At the time of his visit to Indiana, I still had the office in Anderson. He had a couple of areas on his skin that looked very suspicious for skin cancers. Family members had been trying to convince him to have them evaluated. He decided somewhat abruptly that if I would do the work for him, he would consent to have them biopsied. I had a pretty nice procedure room in my little office. I took him there, and I simply froze a couple of sun-damaged areas. Three of the bigger and more worrisome looking places were removed to be sent to pathology to be analyzed for possible cancer. Before we got everything done, I bet he asked me a dozen times if I had ever done a procedure like that.

"Yes, Grandpa. Many times," I tried to allay his concerns repeatedly. Finally exasperated, I said, "No Grandpa, but I read about it in a book last night." That's what he went home and told everybody.

I don't think he could believe that I truly was a doctor. He would frequently start conversations with me this way. "Doug, you're 'sorty' a doctor, ain't you?" There was never any humorous tone in that inquiry. He wanted to make sure his questions were being answered with a modicum of expertise. I shouldn't feel bad, though. We were not sure he ever knew my brother's name. He always referred to him as "that other boy."

11

How's Your Cargo?

Without doubt, the happiest experience for Laura and me while I was in practice in Anderson was the birth of our first daughter. We were married six years before we got the monkey and our parents off our backs. We had gone through one miscarriage. We waited just a little while when we found out she was pregnant again before spreading the news. When we were pretty sure this one was going to "take," we told everybody. Not a soul was unaware: family, friends, neighbors, mailmen, paper boys, and yes, my patients were updated regularly. The patients would hear the latest news from me, and each had to recount the update to my nurse, assistant, and office manager. By the end of the day, my poor staff didn't want to hear any more. "Dr. Smith's wife is having a baby. Whoop-de-do!" I have become a little more reserved in my old age, but back then I lived my life entirely on my sleeve for the world to see.

Sometime right after the due date, for about three days,

Laura busied herself with the most unusual tasks. Among others, she decided the drapes needed to be dusted and the cabinets needed to be rearranged. I guess humans do still have instincts. I think in some way she was "nesting." Finally, one day, shortly after I left home for morning rounds, Laura started having contractions. Later in the morning after she had spoken with her obstetrician, Dr. Joe Copeland (a true hero), she went to Labor and Delivery. I completed my rounds at the hospital, went to the office to see the few early patients we did not have a chance to cancel, and I started to notice a little tickle in my throat. While I was at the office, my office manager, Judy, went to be our surrogate labor coach until I could make it. By the time I got there about noon, things were progressing, but slowly.

The decision was made to give Laura the medicine oxytocin to augment her contractions. Mid-afternoon turned into evening, and I was coughing. Dang it. I almost never got sick. Here was one of the most important days of my life, and I had to hack it up. I would hold my breath as she endured a contraction, and then I would cough in paroxysms until it was time to do it all over again. I suggested that I might step out just for a minute to get some medicine, but she forbade me to leave. I guess a wife has the right to dictate her husband's whereabouts during the labor process. At least, mine did.

We decided a few weeks earlier that we did not want anyone else hanging around with us during this little journey. Laura's parents lived about thirty miles away in Carmel, IN, and my parents lived in our town. Of course, we let them know that Laura was actively engaged in the business of producing a grandchild for them. We said we would call them with good news soon. Fortunately, my brother and sister-in-law were not great at following directions. They showed up after dinner to check on us, and I was so thankful that they did. They went and retrieved some cough medicine for me.

After my cough had eased and we had sent TD and Cheryl on their way, we concentrated on our original objective. The oxytocin had been incrementally increased, and the labor pattern was good. The monitor showed nicely spaced, symmetrical, deep contractions. The baby's heartbeat was continuously monitored. It would decrease in concert with a contraction and return to normal as the contraction eased. This pattern of matched decelerations was perfectly normal. Despite this nice labor pattern, things were still progressing slowly. Ultimately we were just dealing with the old square-peg, round-hole phenomenon. The baby was not fitting through the birth canal. With unwavering determination, Laura kept after it, and I was content just to not cough.

At one point late in the evening, another contraction started that seemed routine. As the monitor displayed the usual peak, Laura let out a blood-curdling war-whoop that was entirely different from what had become her usual expression of discomfort that may or may not have been laced with a little profanity. This bellow shook the windows. Simultaneously, the baby's heartbeat fell precipitously. Almost immediately, my perception of the events to follow changed. I became a bystander, almost looking down on a slow motion film with distorted audio. Dr. Copeland had not strayed far. He was obviously aware of the change because he entered the room pulling on gloves. Laura's doctor, also a very good friend, told her he was giving her one chance to deliver the baby right there, right then. "Push," he demanded. For reasons that we would understand later, that push was feeble. Immediately, with the help of the nurse who had been caring for Laura, Dr. Joe pushed Laura's bed down the hall, and we literally, in Technicolor television style, burst through double doors into a surgical suite for a true emergency Cesarean-section. As I existed there in that time warp of near completely suspended animation, I was vaguely aware that things were moving at breakneck speed. While the nursing staff prepared for the procedure with expert efficiency, they also talked to me. I think I answered appropriately. I'm not sure. This was not just another case on another day in the everyday life of our hospital. At one point, the anesthesiologist took a second to reassure me, "Everything will be okay." Perhaps it was pallor, trembling, or maybe just a look of uncertainty in my eyes that belied my true emotional state. To this day, I still vividly remember that brief expression of kindness and encouragement. Thank you, Dr. Romero.

Laura was asleep, and Joe was poised with a scalpel over her abdomen. He gave me the briefest glance and began. He expertly performed an operation that was second nature for him. He gave concise commentary as he worked. When he entered the peritoneal cavity, the space that houses all of the organs of the abdomen and pelvis, I heard him say, "Blood.

Suction." I saw blood coursing up the suction tubing to the canister on the wall. For a fleeting moment, I envisioned a horrible trajectory for my life. I briefly saw an existence that left me not only childless but widowed as well. Suddenly, Joe's efforts did not seem so meticulous anymore, and my thoughts were redirected from the future back into the moment. It seemed like he literally tore Laura's uterus open. He pulled out this big-footed, spiky-haired, blue blob and passed it off to one of the two nurses standing by to care for the infant. He then turned his attention to finding the source of the bleeding. As he did, he said, "Dr. Smith, why don't you help resuscitate that baby?"

Seriously? At that moment, my ability to maintain an upright position was in jeopardy. Somehow without falling, I was able to walk to the resuscitation station where the nurses were drying, rubbing, and supplying a little oxygen to blow by the baby's nose and mouth. I can't say when, in that whole sequence of events, I truly realized the baby was our daughter. That foreboding blue color was giving way to the pink of life in a little girl whom I was supposed to hold, hug, tickle, send to college, laugh and cry with, and love for the rest of my life. For the briefest moment, I wasn't able to think like a clinician. I wasn't a doctor at all; I was just a husband and a dad.

Fortunately, my role in the resuscitation was to simply watch as the two skilled nurses expertly stimulated our daughter to vigorous life. There is a grading system, called the Apgar score, that is used to assess the well-being of a newborn baby. Scores of zero to two are assigned to five categories — appearance, pulse, grimace, activity, and respiration at one and five minutes respectively. You would think Doctor Dad would recall the one-minute Apgar score. Not the case. I did recover my faculties by the five minute mark. I remember she was a nine at five minutes. I thought her going from looking like a squid at one minute to an Apgar score of nine at five minutes was prophetic of a bright future. Of course I thought that; I was her dad.

By the time the baby, now known as Jeri, was dry, warm, and pink, the surgical team had discovered the cause of the near catastrophe. The uterus, that muscular organ that houses a developing fetus and then expels him or her into the outside world, has supporting structures called ligaments that help hold it in place. When Laura caterwauled, the uterus had ruptured. As when any muscle is torn, it bled profusely. Here is where I talk about God's grace. Most of the bleeding went directly into one of those supports called the broad ligament. That caused pressure that helped to naturally slow the flow of blood. If the bleeding had occurred anywhere else, it could have continued unabated, free-flowing. Laura could have bled to death right there in front of me. That fleeting premonition I had about leaving that operating suite alone was almost a reality.

Dr. Copeland was able to stabilize Laura's condition very quickly. After she was transferred to her room, she slept the rest of that night and most of the next day. She was lightly snoring when Jeri, who had been sleeping in a portable crib next to her bed, popped her eyes open. I was blown away by the look of curiosity and intelligence in that newborn human being's eyes. I fed her for this first of many late-night feedings. That would become the natural divide in the workload that Laura and I would have for a long time. I would do late nights, and she would take early mornings.

Jeri was back in the nursery, and after assuring a somewhat concerned nursing staff that she would be fully attentive to this baby tomorrow, Laura slumbered on. (Laura is a wonderful mother. The rigors of a long labor, blood loss, and an emergency C-section had rendered her briefly incapacitated.) Sometime well after midnight, there was a knock at the door. Our friend, Dr. Bixler, looked through a crack in the door, and I waved him in. He carried a pizza box and had a small backpack over one shoulder. Without saying anything, he squinted back through a narrow slit in the doorway several times. Finally, he seemed satisfied with his surveillance. He pulled beers out of the backpack. The cold pizza and the lukewarm beer and the fact that he brought Bud Light (his brand, not mine), did not detract from a fantastic celebration. At one point, Laura woke briefly from her morphine-assisted respite and shared a couple of carefully-monitored sips of beer. The forbidden nature of that little clandestine party made it all the more enjoyable. It was the perfect finale to, well... a pretty cool day.

The next day I saw a couple of patients I had in the hospital, and I visited in the doctors' lounge for a long time before heading home to shower and shave. I made a couple, okay, maybe a half dozen or so phone calls, before I headed back to the hospital. When I made it back, I was floored by the sight and smell of Laura's room. We had told every person we knew that we were having a baby, and I think every single one of them sent flowers. The only places I have seen collections of flowers like that are Disney World and the funeral home. That outpouring of love and support was a little overwhelming. We asked the nursing staff to give flowers to other patients who might enjoy them. One of my oldest friends, David Bratton, visited that day. I had known him since we played Little League baseball together, and he was my first college roommate. A friendship that long-standing offers a lot of persuasive power. I was able to convince him to take a planter home.

When he protested, "Damn, Dougie, I'm supposed to bring flowers." I stuck another basket in his arms.

I think two days after delivery, I drove a carload of those flowers to our house and returned to take Laura, Jeri, and the remaining plants home. It was early April and still pretty cold. I pulled my car up to the entry and left it running with the heater on. A volunteer pushed Laura in a wheelchair, and I carried Jeri in her car seat. As we approached the car, I set Jeri down briefly to assist Laura with getting in the car. When I turned my attention back to Jeri, I saw with horror that I had positioned her so that the car's exhaust was blowing directly on her. Great job, Doctor Dad.

As we drove toward our old home and new life, we talked about the future. After a brief silence, I asked Laura, "How's your cargo?" She tightened her forehead and raised her eyebrows in a little bit of a perplexed expression. Thinking that I was, for some unknown reason, asking about the function of an automobile and not the precious passenger directly behind her, she finally said, "Vroom, vroom." Nice work, Nurse Mom.

Our daughter was doomed.

It would be three years before our second daughter, Erin, was born. Her birth was notable only for the fact that she peed on Dr. Copeland as soon as she was delivered. There was none of the drama we had experienced three years earlier. Because Laura's uterus had been ruptured, Erin was born by repeat C-section. We had decided that two children would be our limit, so Laura prearranged with Dr. Copeland to have her tubes tied after the delivery while all the organs were already exposed. Impromptu, with no preplanning, I asked Dr. Copeland if he could remove Laura's appendix. After all, the anatomy was there wide open, and taking it out might prevent a problem for her in the future. It was during that last part of the procedure that Laura's spinal anesthesia began to wane a little. She started to feel what was going on, and she was not happy with me. Great job, Doctor Husband.

Yes, Bix smuggled in beer to share with Laura later that night, and I'm pretty sure he was fully clothed. At least, Laura never said anything if he wasn't. I was at home with Jeri. The couple of days that Laura and Erin were in the hospital passed without a hiccup. Once again, we drove home and contemplated the future. If we had realized just how many weary days lay ahead of us, Laura and I would have soaked in those couple of nights of sleep with the thankfulness they deserved. Erin would not sleep through the night regularly for three years.

Mom and Dad were doomed.

12

Doing Life

Home with No Call

In the last few years, there has been a lot written about physician burnout and the need for "work-life balance." When I first started in private practice well before I went to work in the Express Care, I truly thought the sixty to eighty-hour work week was a sign of strength and honor. I lasted about six years on that hamster wheel. Back then on call looked like this. I took my own after-hours calls during the week. Friday afternoon until Monday morning was a rotation call. There were six of us in the group. I took my turn, with my mistresses named Pager and Phone, every sixth weekend, and Laura and I crammed as much living into those five free weekends that we possibly could. We socialized. We dabbled in golf and gardening. We watched basketball, and we kept the Miller Brewing Company in business. In order to make ends meet, even if hung over a lot of the time, I still made rounds on my patients who were in the hospital on Saturdays and Sundays. In addition to not wanting to give up that income, I enjoyed hospital work and caring for sicker patients more than office work, and I felt emotionally attached to my patients. I really believed there was value in continuity of care. In the end, what came out of that was I got a reputation for being "dedicated."

"Dedicated" meant that I not only made rounds every weekend, but I left home before my family was awake and got home after they were already in bed. Just as it happens for people in all walks of life, the "cargo" Laura and I brought home from the hospital caused me to reevaluate everything. Having our daughter made me realize I needed more "balance." I remember getting home one night, and Laura was asleep. I stood over Jeri's crib. The dark hair she had when she was born had given way to blonde. She rhythmically worked the pacifier in her mouth as she slept. I had trouble remembering the last time I had seen her awake. I wished she would wake and stretch her little arms up at me, so I could pick her up. It was shortly after that very moment that I made the best decision of my life. I took that Express Care position that offered fixed hours with no call. There is no doubt in my mind that decision saved my career and probably my sanity as well. The demand in my soul that I spend more time with my family was another huge, motivating factor that caused me to make that drastic change in my career.

With the new job, I essentially worked half the days of the year. That included half the weekend days and half the holidays, but I still felt like I had died and gone to heaven. I was home half the time, and did I mention that there was no call? I think being a little older when we finally had kids helped us to appreciate how precious and fleeting time with them really was. Laura and I took full advantage of our time with the girls. I remember when the days lengthened in spring, at least once a year, we would be caught off guard at about eight o'clock in the evening, realizing that we hadn't eaten and homework was not done. Time sneaks up on you when you are hitting softballs, playing badminton, jumping on a pogo stick, taking pony rides, or just having fun. Doing life and caring for my family was the greatest balancing distraction from work.

Moonsville

When our oldest daughter was eight months old, we moved out of town to a small farm in Moonsville, IN. Until she left for college, our youngest daughter, Erin, never lived anywhere else. Moonsville isn't on most maps. It only has one stop sign, and except for residential homes and structures for farming, the only other building is the small, cinder block Conservation Club. That's where I vote, and I have never waited more than a couple of minutes to cast my ballot.

Moonsville is most well known, in my mind anyway, for what I call "The Moonsville Rock Festival That Wasn't." A local group of young entrepreneurs missed the famous Woodstock festival that was held in 1969, and they felt cheated. A year later, they planned a similar event to take place on soybean fields that are just two miles from our home. They already had acts booked and publicity promotions in full swing when the county shut them down. We still point out the location, where the event was supposed to be held, every time we pass by it. I think the girls and I enjoy commemorating a defunct concert because we have found tremendous pleasure in sharing music back and forth over the years. Back when I still stored my playlist on a giant iPod, the girls openly expressed that it would be the one item they would fight over when I die. I'm glad they have come to agree with me and Friedrich Nietzsche that, "Without music, life would be a mistake.[3]"

Besides having an almost daily reminder to enjoy a good tune, living in Moonsville has given us a more rugged lifestyle in which to immerse ourselves. While not for everybody, country living has provided us equilibrium. Caring for horses has been a central theme for us. Feeding them when it's twenty below zero, tending to them when they're sick or injured, and even mucking their stalls has given us a great sense of purpose. Witnessing the personalities these beasts possess has filled us with wonder, and seeing how they bond with people has given us an appreciation for them as living beings that deserve respect.

We also ran cattle for several years. Those fence riding behemoths were a lot of work, and there was never a deep connection like we had with the horses. We pretty much just raised them for beef. One time when Jeri was about five years old, Laura's sister was visiting. She asked Jeri what the cows' names were, and she was appalled when Jeri answered,

---

3 https://www.goodreads.com/author/quotes/1938.Friedrich_Nietzsche

"Breakfast, Lunch, and Supper." The cattle business came to a halt shortly after a sheriff's deputy woke me up early one morning to tell me that some of our cows had been run over by a semi on the county highway. That made me want to find a different way to put meat in the freezer.

Farm living provided great life lessons for our girls as they were growing up. They got to see things kids living in the city often do not. They became familiar with deer, foxes, hawks, groundhogs, herons, beavers, squirrels, chipmunks, and hummingbirds to name a few. Seeing calves born and old horses put down, they experienced the full range of emotions of nature's life cycle.

They also saw that maintaining order on a farm requires diligence, resolve, hard work, and completing some disagreeable duties. We've had a constant battle with some kind of pest out here: weeds, insects, moles, 'possums, raccoons, and skunks. Many people, who have never spent any time out in the country, don't understand that doing battle with those varmints meant we trapped and killed them. Once, I made the mistake of telling a couple of nurses that I shot a 'possum before I came to work that day. I honestly thought they wanted to report me to an agency for animal cruelty or subject me to some other inquisition. They didn't know what it's like to open a shed to find a three-foot mound of raccoon poop, and they never had a neighbor whose horse died because a 'possum crapped on its hay. ('Possums carry a protozoal germ in their feces. If a horse eats hay contaminated with the excrement, the germ can migrate to the horse's brain and kill it.)

Our youngest daughter caught the love of horses from her mom. Equestrian-related activities were her big thing, and we know when she stayed close to home for college, it was not to be near us. She couldn't leave her horses. Usually, the extermination of pests was left up to me, but if I was not available, our sweet, diminutive Erin had no issue with protecting her horses. If that meant a 22 to a marsupial's head...well, she didn't like it, but she would do it.

For some reason, the first time Erin was required to perform that unpleasant task, Laura posted about it all over social media, only she made a typo. The O and the I are right next to each other on the keyboard (shot/shit). How could such a little girl have defecated an animal? The jokes abounded.

Emotions aside, it was a job that had to be done, and the girls saw more examples of situations that required whatever it took. Once, a baby calf got his head stuck in a two trunked, V-shaped tree on the back of our property. He would have died if we had been unable to get him loose. He had breached a small opening in a fence to get back to that treeline. The mother cow could not squeeze through, and she snorted and paced the fence menacingly, while Laura and I tried to free her baby. We pushed and pulled, and he kicked, bawled, and farted. After much trial and error, we used a long two by four as a lever and the rescue was completed. Even covered in calf slobber and crap, we felt great satisfaction in completing what felt like an honorable mission.

Another time, we could not find anybody to help us put hay in the barn. We had just short of one hundred bales on the ground, and a storm was heading our way. If we didn't get the hay up before it got wet, it would be ruined. Some of those bales weighed sixty-five plus pounds, and Laura and I picked up all ninety-eight of them, loaded them on a trailer, and stacked them in the barn in less than two hours. On both of those "must get done" occasions and countless others, we looked at each other and asked, "What do people in the city do?"

The Running Ninja

I do think manual labor, like hefting those hay bales, has helped keep me healthy over the years, but it didn't provide a regular diversion for me. Exercise is a great escape for many. I know several people in medicine who are cyclists, triathletes, and CrossFit enthusiasts. For many years, I let myself make the excuse that I was too busy to exercise. I was in my late-forties when I started two activities at about the same time. I started running and training for American Ninja Warrior (ANW).

I have said this about ANW. People have one of two reactions when they first see that show. "Those people are nuts," or "I have to try that." I fell into the latter category, and I still cannot explain why. I started with basic things: push-ups, sit-ups, pull up bar, treadmill, and free weights. Then I started running outside. I built obstacles in my backyard: warped wall, salmon ladder, quad steps. I ran in mud run obstacle course competitions. After about a year of training, I sent in an audition video to ANW. I honestly thought I had a shot at getting on the show. I was old. I was a doctor. I had just enough skill that I might be able to make a decent showing. They are always looking for a good story. I was right. I got a chance in two consecutive seasons.

First, I flew out to Venice Beach and the next year to Dallas. I wish I could tell you that I lit it up. Miserably, I hit the water on the very first obstacle both times. At Venice Beach, I slogged the half mile back to my hotel in wet shoes and kicked myself with every step. I became convinced that I had to try one more time. I trained harder and submitted an even better application video. The next year, I was tagged for an interview in Dallas. I was whisked away from a group of newly formed friends and fellow competitors to meet with one of the editors of the show. I was filmed for a personal interest piece. When the show aired, I was featured as the first participant of the day. I was actually about one hundred twenty-seventh to run the course. After I got on the start platform, there was a long delay. No less than ten minutes elapsed before the start tone launched my run. There was one little problem. My heart had been pounding, ringing in my ears the entire time I stood in the wings. I was spent. I took a swim on the first obstacle, quad steps, something I could do in my sleep.

Disappointed, yes, but I was mostly embarrassed. I was still working in the Emergency Department when I was doing ANW. The staff put up a big banner wishing me good luck before I left for Dallas. I had to go back and tell them that I let them down. It would be a long time before I could take anything positive, except for the friends I made, out of the experience. Fast forward eleven years. I'm now coaching high school basketball. I teach kids techniques that I have learned to help prevent them from choking the way I did.

The elites of ANW have a superhuman level of physical fitness. I only made it to the average old guy Ninja level, but I have been able to retain a fair amount of it—still water skiing at age sixty. Just the other day, I did the AC/DC "Thunderstruck," high plank/low plank exercise challenge with my high school athletes. There was only one person still planking at the end of that four-minute, fifty-two-second song. Maybe the old coach applied that stubborn streak of his in a good way that time.

I fared a little better in the running department. Some background might help with perspective. Where we live, exercise is not a priority for most of our neighbors. Some of the farmers feel like they get enough physical activity with their work, but many just prefer a sedentary lifestyle. They enjoy peace, ease, and comfort with a smoke and big double-sized soda from the quick-mart. More than once while I was running, someone pulled up beside me in his car or truck, laughed, and asked, "You need a ride, Doc?" Despite not having the social support of a running group, or training partners, after a year and half of running for exercise, I completed a marathon. Under four hours, baby!

Teacher

One source of distraction from the usual demands of the office and hospital actually came with part of the job. Throughout my career in medicine, I was able to teach. As a student and resident, I got to help those coming along behind me. In the office, I hosted a couple of students for their month-long Family Medicine rotations. After I got to St. Vincent, there were almost always students and residents with us. For years, I maintained an "education board" on which we displayed new, interesting information from the medical literature as well as summaries of our own unusual cases. From the time I was in grade school until a consultant or colleague would teach me anything about medicine, I have always held teachers in the highest esteem. Teach me anything, and I'm your loyal fan for life. I know I am not supposed to project feelings and emotions, but I often felt that same kind of connection with the students I taught.

Dealing with motivated learners was extremely rewarding. Except for slowing us down, having students rarely caused any problems. They were sometimes frustrated when a patient would give me a different history. Occasionally, they would be disappointed when my assessment or management didn't match theirs, or they needed more help with a procedure than they thought they would. One day shortly after I started in the Express Care, we were extremely busy. I was working with a fourth-year student for the first time. I saw a mechanic who had cut his finger. He didn't have any signs of a more serious injury. I numbed his finger with an injection. While I was gathering supplies, I talked with the student. Yes, she had done lots of sutures. Yes, she felt comfortable. Great, she could stitch while I saw a couple of patients. This man had gotten injured at work, and his wound was dirty. It needed to be irrigated very thoroughly to try to flush out any contamination. Yes, she understood. When I returned to check on things, I was shocked to see that the finger now looked like a bratwurst. I had placed an angiocatheter out to be used for irrigation. It has a flexible plastic sheath that slides over a long needle. That's how an IV is started. For irrigation, the skinny tube is removed from the needle, attached to a syringe, and used like a squirt gun. She hadn't removed the catheter and was sticking the needle part into the wound. By the time, I got back to her, she had injected that finger with 20 cc's of saline. To give you an idea, we try to limit ourselves to about 2 cc's of anesthetic when numbing a finger. Too much volume in the limited space in a finger can shut off blood flow. We were able to loosely approximate the edges of the cut. I called that man daily for a week, and I removed his stitches after two weeks. He did fine. Even the pleasant diversion of having students had its moments.

Last Call for Alcohol

Truly significant balance, between the hospital and home, stress and tranquility, would come to me slowly, in a couple of ways, over a few years. You have heard the saying, "Change your mind; change your life." I want to take that a step further. You change your mind by changing your heart. Again, the first step in that process for me was having children. That's when I began to realize that there was a priority even more important to me than seeing patients. Maybe medicine didn't completely define who I was. If I failed at that, I had other hats to wear.

The next part of the process was ditching alcohol. Laura and I both came from families with a history of alcohol abuse, and I had seen in my patients the shattered dreams and total devastation that drugs and alcohol could cause. Even with that experience and understanding, we both looked to Lite beer as that magic elixir, guaranteed to make you have fun and relieve all the stress in the world. Predictably, it did neither. It only made things worse. We would sometimes rationalize, even together, that neither of us missed work, had DUI's, or got injured while inebriated, but pointing all that out was just self-justification for something both of us knew was keeping us from being our best. Feeling bad from Friday and Saturday nights, I wouldn't read and study on Sunday the way I knew I should. After a few too many, Laura and I would often argue and say some really hurtful things to one another, me more to her than she to me. I am pretty sure it was on my thirtieth birthday that, in front of my good friend, David, I called the woman who means more to me than anything in the world, who has stood by me through thick and thin, who takes care of our children, who is a beloved school nurse, and who dotes over my elderly parents, a "piece of shit." David told me that blow up caused his stomach to hurt. Thinking about that moment thirty years later still makes me feel sick. I caused pain for others around me too. My brother walked off the golf course once to avoid punching me in the whiskey mouth. Adding guilt and regret to an already pressured existence only added to the misery.

After I changed schedules and started to work late at night, Laura found herself drinking nightly after she put the girls to bed. She was self-aware enough to realize that her consumption was escalating, and that really scared her. So, she did something about it. She quit, and there was a voice like a whisper in my ears telling me I needed to follow her lead. At first, I tried to save face with my beer-swilling pals by saying I needed to support Laura. Drinking in front of her wouldn't be right. Really, I was relieved. The farce was over. I knew I had been robbing myself of massive potential — potential to be a good husband, father, son, brother, friend, and doctor.

There was no Koala Center or any formal or informal treatment. I just stopped throwing cases of Lite beer in the cart at the grocery, and I passed by the liquor store. I even went to Meadowbrook Pizza and drank soda. I became the designated driver for our annual Indianapolis 500 get together that I have been a part of for nearly forty years. This is one place I can say with unwavering certainty, that being stubborn was truly a benefit. I said, "I quit." That was the end of it.

The Hound of Heaven

About the same time we became teetotalers, we decided to send Jeri to a private school. We chose Anderson Christian School (ACS), but we didn't choose ACS for its religious teaching. It was the smaller size and more personalized instruction that appealed to us. The building was shared by Lindberg Road Church of Christ, and it was located just a few blocks from where we lived when we first moved back to Anderson. Because of its less than glamorous architectural style, we always called it "the warehouse church." Now we were sending our daughter to school there, and soon, at the urging of Jeri's kindergarten teacher, Laura started going to church services there as well.

I did not jump on that ride as quickly as I had the booze-less express. I had it figured out. There was no way a God, at least not as "they" portrayed Him, could exist. All the church people I had ever heard said God was omnipotent and loving, but how could that be? After all, the world was full of violence, hunger, hatred, and illness. Would God really let sick children die? I wasn't buying any of it, but I eventually went to show Laura that I supported and respected her decision.

I didn't go with any regularity at first, but I started to enjoy seeing some really nice people, and there was that whispering voice again, urging me to go and listen. Randy Wood was the preacher. He was genuine, down to earth, and a fantastic speaker. After attending a few Sundays, I began to wonder why anyone else was there. The messages seemed to be pointedly focused directly at me.

I can't explain what was happening. I felt this vague but constant urging to put those messages in my heart. Finally, one day I was at home alone. Laura was at work. Jeri was at school, and Erin was with the babysitter. I had been working outside and came into our mudroom to get a bottle of water. Standing there in front of the refrigerator, I heard the voice again. Only this time, it was not a whisper. The voice was firm, distinct, and unmistakably that of Jesus Christ. This is the strangest part. I can't tell you the exact words that I heard that day, but the message was crystal clear. It was time for me to get off the sidelines and get in the game. Imagination, hallucination, hearing something I just wanted to hear? I didn't think so then, and I still don't believe it was any of those things. I wasn't meditating or even thinking about Randy's sermons when that message came to me. I left a little early to pick Jeri up at school and stopped by Randy's office. I got baptized that evening.

I recounted that story to one of my friends later. He just smiled and said, "You were being pursued by the hound of heaven." Psalm 9:10. No, I still don't know the "why" behind wars and sickness, but I do know what I experienced in my mudroom a few years back was as real as the rising sun.

The changing of my heart, changing my mind, and changing my life is still a work in progress. Steadily, I have come to think of things very differently. The way I started to approach patients is just one example. I always tried to care for patients with caring, efficiency, and effectiveness, but my motives were not always the purest. Sometimes I was more focused on efficiency because I wanted to make more money. I was determined to be effective because I didn't want to get sued. I wanted to be caring, but I still allowed myself to feel irritated at patients when their ill-timed illnesses or injuries inconvenienced me. I haven't perfected the attitudes that accompany a servant's heart, but I can tell you that I do feel and think about, not only patients, but everybody, including myself, differently, and that has given me a feeling of balance in all that I do.

I'm happy to discuss faith issues with anybody who might be interested. Hit me up at SortofaDoctor@gmail.com.

13

Doctoring at Home

We were taught in medical school that we shouldn't take care of our family members. We're too close and can't be objective. A lot of docs will say they don't provide medical care for their families, and most who say that are being less than honest. I provided care and treatment for my family many times, and I saw my colleagues do the same. I drew the line when anything seemed more serious, and I never prescribed a controlled substance for any of them.

I treated the girls for their multiple ear infections when they were small. I also stitched Laura up at the kitchen table one time when she cut her hand. Just as it was a bad idea for us to work together, the same was true about me doctoring her. The numbing wasn't done with the gentleness that she thought it should have been. Rather than directly providing their care as I did with that ill-conceived suturing procedure, I more commonly just gave insight to their providers and offered support.

After I left private practice, I worked the second shift, 11 a.m. to 11 p.m., noon or 2 p.m. to 10 p.m. When the girls got older, they wanted to call almost every night that I worked to tell me goodnight. It became a game with our unit secretaries and nurses who answered the phone. Jeri was usually the one to initiate the calls, and she would always ask, "Is my daddy busy?"

Teasing her, they would reply, "I don't know. Who's your daddy?" On one occasion, the girls were staying with their godparents, Mike and Cindy. Laura was at a Bible study, and her phone was dead. Jeri made what seemed like her usual call three times over about an hour and a half. I was busy each time she called. About the same time the unit secretary told me that Jeri had called several times, Laura called. She was able to retrieve frantic messages from Mike and Cindy when she got home and plugged her phone in. Turns out Jeri was calling to let me know that Erin had crashed a go-cart into a giant concrete planter. She cut her lip and knocked out three permanent teeth.

Erin received excellent emergency dental care that night from Mike and Cindy's dentist and friend. The next day, Laura attended to Erin while I was at work. On the second day post injury, Laura and I were concerned because our patient was not drinking. I had to go to the bank, and I told Laura that if she couldn't get her to take fluids by the time I got home, we would arrange for her to be admitted for IV fluids. When I got back, maybe two sips had made it past those parched and swollen lips. Here was one place where membership had its benefits. I was able to call Erin's physician, Dr. Jerry Irwin, directly. He had been in my call group when I was in private practice. He was a confidant, a trusted resource, and he was my friend. He admitted Erin himself, and we were able to bypass the Emergency Department. I was sitting on the couch next to Erin when I talked to her doctor. After I ended the call, she pointed to the tablet we had been using to communicate with her. It hurt her too much to talk. I watched as she slowly wrote these words: Am — I — going — to — die?

My heart broke at that moment. It hurt me to know that my daughter had such fear. Those emotions occurred for us when we were certain she would be fine. I can't begin to imagine what a family endures when a child with cancer asks the same question.

I don't think kids actually keep a scorecard, but it seems like they don't want their siblings to "one-up" them in the injury or illness department. In this regard, Jeri has definitely been our over-achiever. We had an old, glass aquarium in the barn, and she decided to use it as a step stool one day. When it broke through, it sliced her foot. It is probably best that I was at work in Indy that night. I probably would have had two in the family, she and Laura, who did not appreciate my suturing skill. However, as she grew older, I became her first consultant for any medical issue. When she was in college, I met her early, before one of my shifts at the hospital, to remove an ingrown toenail for her.

Another time when she was younger, she fell off the monkey bars at school and broke her arm. Again, I was able to grease the system a little, and my friend, Dr. Bert Davis, straightened the broken bones (medically it's called a reduction) and applied a cast. This was done in Surgery under anesthesia. The only story here is what the aftereffects of anesthesia and an unreserved personality might combine to do. After the procedure, she was kept very briefly in the Recovery Room, and then she was transferred to Pediatrics for a little more observation. It didn't take long before she was pacing and standing in the doorway of her room. She kept demanding, "Daddy, please just get our bill, so we can go home."

Jeri was the central figure in what we consider as a family to be the biggest hardship we have endured to date. Laura and the girls are Disney nuts. Just before Jeri's senior year in high school, we took a trip to Disney World. As we were traveling home, she started to cough. She already had a little tendency to have a deeper cough that lasted a little longer than most people would have with a cold or bronchitis. At first, this cough seemed similar to her previous episodes. She saw her pulmonologist, Dr. Saiful Kabir. He treated her as though she had bronchospasm, but after her initial visit things got worse. A few days later, I took her back to his office. My brother is a pharmaceutical rep, and he saw us in the parking lot. He, the other patients in the waiting room, and Dr. Kabir's staff were horrified. This cough was unlike anything any of us had previously seen. It was deep, from the toes. It was so hard it made my own ribs hurt to watch it, and it was non-stop. Dr. Kabir admitted her to the hospital that day for testing and to try to get her some relief. My dad came to see her. He said that when he left, he prayed for the first time he could remember. He was afraid she was going to die.

In the old days, whooping cough was referred to as "The Hundred Days Cough," and that's about how long it lasted for Jeri. She coughed eighteen to twenty hours a day for a little over three months. The condition starts with a bacterial infection. After about a week the patient is really no longer contagious. The lining of the airways in the lungs has been damaged and has to regenerate and repair itself before the cough will cease. The textbooks say there is no effective treatment for the hacking that is caused by whooping cough. I can tell you that the textbooks are one hundred percent correct.

Being around someone who is coughing stirs a lot of emotions- concern, compassion, frustration, even annoyance. Once, I went into our bedroom, and I noticed the door to the bathroom was closed. I heard the fans running, but I didn't hear the shower. I thought one of us had forgotten to turn the fans off. I opened the door to find Laura sitting on the floor. She looked up, shrugged, and burst into tears.

Jeri tried to return to school when she was no longer contagious, but she was kicked out because her cough was so disruptive. She studied at home for the entire semester. I served as a study partner for the AP Physics class she was taking. Except for trying to help her with school work and being as positive as I could be, there was little I could do.

She might have inherited the tendency to rewatch a movie over and over again from one of her parents. Her go-to for that period of her life was "How the Grinch Stole Christmas."

When I turned in our drive at night after my trip home from work, I would see the Grinch on our television through the windows in our sunroom. All her physician father had to offer was to rub her back and watch Jim Carrey with her until we both fell asleep. I began to pray as I drove home that there would be no Grinch when I turned in the drive. Eventually, there wasn't.

14

Express Care

Impostor

Looking after my family spanned my entire career and still goes on today. My search for balance in life escalated when I was drowning in private practice. Things definitely improved as soon as I started what would ultimately be twenty-two years working in the Express Care, but finding a peaceful existence was a gradual process. I knew the transition from private practice in a smaller town to working in the Emergency Department in a city like Indianapolis was going to be a challenge. The pace was much quicker. I don't want to say the patients were not as nice as my old patients, but the relationship was entirely different. Many of my old patients were people I had known my entire life. They were more like family. I did not know any of the patients I was seeing in this new practice setting. The volume was such that people often had to wait a long time before they were seen. That made them mad, and that made me nervous.

All this change resurrected an old malady. When you know, intellectually, you have been well schooled and trained for some task or occupation, but your mind and emotions tell you that you are unfit for duty, it can make for a disconcerted spirit. I sparred with Impostor Syndrome, off and on my entire life. When I first started classes in undergraduate studies at Indiana University, I was not sure my high school had prepared me to meet the academic demands of university. I was nearly paralyzed with fear when I first started medical school. I knew for sure that I was a charlatan when I first started seeing patients in my private practice.

A memory from my intern year at Ball Memorial Hospital has found permanent lodging in my mind. Although my first clinical rotation there was a general Internal Medicine service, my first overnight call was in the Intensive Care Unit. The day was finished, but the night was just beginning. I walked through the automatic electric doors into the ICU. As the doors closed behind me, my rear simultaneously slammed shut in an autonomous spasm that told me I should turn around and run. Was I covering the ICU overnight? I was a complete phony.

Somehow, despite near suffocating anxiety, I made it through that first call night. The first day I would officially see patients in private practice, I arrived at the office about forty-five minutes early. As time passed, my heart rate got faster and faster. I was going to shake hands with my first patient and tell him that I was his new doctor. I survived each and every one of those self-created ordeals. With age and maturity, those feelings and thoughts have become much less pervasive, but even now they occasionally try to poke their way into my consciousness.

Reading about Impostor Syndrome and learning to recognize it for what it was helped me to deal with it. It is another extension of being type-A, obsessive-compulsive. Those traits, in moderation, can be desirable for a physician because they cause him or her to be meticulous and thorough, but they can also be the piper at the gate leading one to disaster. Those pieces of a person's mental and emotional character can push him over the edge. From the time I first started in medicine, I had always been teetering on that precipice, sure that inadequacy would propel me down the slope of discovery into public shame. I was banking on a change in venue, a new direction in my career, to help me prevent that slide.

Fortunately, the people who hired me were fantastic. All were willing to answer questions and help me. One doctor in particular, Dr. Louis Profeta, went out of his way to aid me in the transition. Maybe it does go back to my childhood days as a student, and I know I expressed it previously. I have always had a deep appreciation for those who took the interest and initiative to teach me anything. This was way more than "anything." This was my career, and it was treating patients. The generous support from Dr. Profeta and the rest of the group was everything to me.

I also realized pretty quickly that I, with my own mix of personality traits, was better suited for this kind of practice. I was forced to make definitive decisions on the spot. Labs, x-ray results, and EKG's had to be interpreted in real-time. Charts had to be completed before I left. I'm not saying I didn't think about cases when I left, but physically carrying work home with me was not an option. When I was off, I was truly off.

Triage

There was another challenge in the transition into this new practice. Triage comes from the French word *trier* meaning to sort, and in medicine, triage is a little tricky and far from perfect. Triage is the process that places patients in the hierarchy of care, the pecking order, who goes first, and where they are seen. As a physician trained in Family Medicine, I took on a new role as a doctor in the area called the Express Care. The idea was that those of us who worked in that area would see more minor emergency cases, and that was mostly true. However, the initial description of problems could often be very misleading. Patients presented with concerns, and their emotions were frequently running very high. Sometimes patients subconsciously manipulated symptoms to fit a preformed notion they had about their condition. They might think their symptoms matched a diagnosis their uncle had or that they read about on the Internet. Other times, patients flat out lied because of embarrassment, to try to get drugs, or to manipulate facts for financial gain. These are just some of the things that made triage a less than ideal process.

Early in my tenure with the new group, I saw a young kid, six years old I think, who had Kawasaki Disease (KD). That condition is an inflammatory process that affects the blood vessels. If not recognized and treated properly it can lead to, among other things, heart problems. It was not something that would usually have been triaged to Express Care. It is pretty rare, so it wasn't immediately thought of when a kid presented with fever and a rash. That was the problem. The presenting symptoms of KD mimic much more common and less serious viral infections that will simply run their course.

Somehow, doing what I was trained to do, which was to make that diagnosis, gave me some credibility with my new group. One of the long-standing partners in the group was Dr. Bob Lew. Dr. Lew had a reputation for being a good and efficient emergency physician. He was also known to have a stern disposition. As I was leaving at the end of that shift in which we had sent the child with Kawasaki Disease upstairs, Dr. Lew stopped me.

Slightly raising his eyebrows in question he said, "Kawasaki in the Express Care, Doctor?"

"I guess that's how it goes sometimes," I answered. He replied with an almost imperceptible nod, and it briefly looked as though he might grin.

That small sign of approval was huge. Maybe it was all in my head, but I seemed to be more accepted and respected after that. That little boost in confidence helped stave off the negative thoughts that were trying to permeate my brain. I had been constantly wondering if I had made a terrible mistake by closing my own practice and going there to work. In time, I would come to recognize that move as one of the best decisions of my life, but for a while the struggle was real. Self-doubt and the fear of failure can drag a person down into the depths if he is not careful.

Over the years, there were many more cases that snuck through triage. Some of the problems we encountered in that 20' by 30' Express Care room with eight cart beds separated by curtains included a couple of heart attacks, a ruptured spleen, blood clots in the legs, a collapsed lung, and penetrating eye trauma. With a running backdrop of thousands of colds, sprains, and minor lacerations that we cared for regularly, we had to be alert to recognize these more immediately critical conditions, and I am thankful that we were not so mind-numb that we forgot to consider unusual diagnoses. I say "we," because our nurses were excellent and their input was invaluable to me and to our patients. Medical practice is a team sport.

From the time patients enter Triage at the front of the Emergency Department, they are placed in a tracking system. Today that is done on computers. In the old days, it was done on a big, white dry erase board. The board had information about the patient's status and location within the department, such as abdominal pain— in x-ray, and of course, it showed where the patient was to be seen.

Fishing

That tracking board was located in the main department, but we could see it through a doorway that led into the Express Care area. One day a patient was slated to be seen by us. The problem was noted to be "fishhook." Shortly after this was posted and before the fishhook patient was called into our treatment area, another patient was assigned for us to see, and the problem was, again, "fishhook." Being located in central Indiana, we did not see fishhook injuries all that often. Having two back to back was unheard of. The mystery was solved when the first patient was called back. He had one of the treble hooks of a lure embedded in his finger. I followed the lure with my eyes to discover that one of the other treble hooks was embedded in his buddy's finger. Trying to help his friend, he had impaled himself. These two goofy old guys were laughing and having a grand old time. This was one of those times I just had to join in the moment. As we creatively worked out a successful plan to separate Mutt and Jeff, I wondered what they would look like mounted above a fish's fireplace.

Another time the board simply said "nasal injury." Most often that meant a person was struck in the nose by a door, a ball, or a fist. This man was a professional bass fisherman. Those guys go a hundred miles an hour going from one location on the lake to another to try to find the best spots. He had gotten his line hung on a snag. When he hastily and with all the force he could muster tried to pull loose, the hook broke off the line and shot long end straight up his nose. The odds are astronomical for that to happen. He should have bought a lottery ticket. He was able simply to pull the hook out with his fingers right after it happened. He came to the Emergency Department because he had the strong sensation that there was still something up in his nose. He was convinced that the lead weight sinker that had been on the line next to the hook was nestled near his brain. Despite an examination displaying only swollen nasal membranes and a negative x-ray, that would have shown a bright white circle had a lead weight been in his nose, this man had difficulty believing that there was nothing else high up in his nasal passage. He felt like something was still there.

I had to exercise a skill that most people do not associate with medicine to reassure that guy. Salesmanship is a cornerstone of the delivery of medical care. I often told students and residents that I should have sold sand in the desert, but nobody would have been fishing there. What fun would that have been?

Glue

Memories seem to get organized in clusters. Like the bunching that occurred in my mind for triage and fishing stories, I have also stored a couple in there for tissue adhesive. Skin glue was developed during the Vietnam war era. It was not used widely in clinical practice until the mid-1990's, not too long after I joined the ER group. About that same time, the Nurse Manager of the Emergency Department talked me into doing a weekly medical segment on the morning news show at Fox. That meant I got up very early once a week and drove to Indianapolis to give a brief demonstration covering some medical topic of the day. Once, we demonstrated the effectiveness of helmets for bicyclists by using watermelons. That episode and the one where I used skin glue to seal up hot dogs that we cut up got the best reviews of any of the things that I did there. I can't remember how long I did the news segments. I enjoyed feeling like I was providing a public service by helping to educate people about important medical issues, but the logistics didn't work so well. If I was scheduled to work the same day I appeared on the show, I would have to leave my house before 6 a.m. and get home after midnight. Since there was no pay and I didn't need to promote a practice, the feeling of doing a good deed was not enough for me to continue in my role as a talking head. I learned some about television, and if one kid ever struck his helmet-protected head instead of his bare skull on the pavement, then I consider that time spent well worth it.

Somewhere in that same time period, I saw a young girl who had broken her ankle. I placed her in a fiberglass splint. Within minutes, her dad brought her back because the splint was rubbing and bothering her. I saw the problem immediately. When the fiberglass hardened, it formed a corner that was poking her. I walked them back into the treatment room where we had just been and took the splint off. I carried it across the room to the cart that held the fiberglass and the large scissors we used to cut the soft fiberglass. The fix was easy. All I needed to do was to snip off that little corner, pad it, and presto. I used the scissors on the cart, and it proved to be a little more difficult than expected. I slipped once with the shears. Undeterred, I tried again. This time I was not only successful in removing the point that was protruding from the splint, but

I also stabbed the pad of my left index finger with the scissors. I simply grabbed a couple of paper towels and applied pressure to my own wound. I assured the patient and her dad that I was fine, and we would have them out of there shortly.

Sarah was the nurse on duty with me that shift. As I have mentioned, the nurses there were excellent. Sarah was no exception, but she never did anything quietly. She was in our main evaluation area, and I was down a very short hallway in our treatment room. I called to her three or four times before she answered.

"What?" she finally called back.

"Come here."

"What for? What do you need?"

"Please come here, and bring some skin glue."

"Skin glue. Oh, for God's sake. What's going on?" she broadcast to everyone.

When she joined us, I continued to hold pressure on my finger, and she reapplied the modified splint to the little girl's foot and ankle. It fit perfectly. It didn't rub anymore. The child was happy, and the dad seemed eager to leave an episode of medical bloopers behind. They left in a hurry.

After they were gone, we turned our attention to my finger. I irrigated the wound and patted it dry. Sarah was laughing at me as she applied the skin glue vigorously. The laceration was closed with the first application and the bleeding stopped. We waited about a minute, and she put another coat on for good measure. Mission accomplished. Everything looked great. I would cover it with a bandaid and wear a glove.

There was only one problem. I held my injured index finger and my middle finger together as Sarah put the glue in place. More than a little glue had run down between those two fingers. My fingers were literally stuck together with super glue.

Annoyed at myself, I sent Sarah on to try to do what she could to get us back on track. Triage had continued to send us patients while this was going on.

Tissue adhesive is oil-soluble, which means it will eventually dissolve in something that is oil-based. I massaged and rubbed and poked Bacitracin ointment into the crease between the two tethered fingers for more than twenty minutes before I could finally separate them. They were sore, but at least they were apart, and the cut was still closed.

Embarrassed and behind, I muddled through the rest of that shift. At the end of the night, I was getting ready to head home. Sarah and I looked at one another and burst out laughing. We laughed until our sides hurt. What else could we do?

Not always routine...thankfully

St. Vincent opened the Peyton Manning Children's Hospital after I had been with the group for about eight years. That caused us to shift Express Care to the St. Vincent Hospital in Carmel, IN. For a short while after that change, I worked part-time for the group while dabbling in some other things. I worked solo coverage in a small Emergency Department in Winchester, IN. I was the Medical Director of an urgent care facility in Anderson. It didn't take long for me to make it back to the SVEP group full time. The fourteen years I worked with that group in Carmel were much like the preceding years, except as a second coverage physician working directly alongside the Emergency Medicine trained doctors of our group, I saw more sick adult patients with medical and surgical problems. The lulling sea of "common" problems that tried to seduce us into missing the truly sick was slightly different there at Carmel. In addition to the upper respiratory infections, the sprains and strains, the back pains, and the lacerations, it also included morbidly obese patients who had complications from their bariatric procedures, including gastric bypasses. Those operations restrict the amount of food the patient can eat because the intestinal tract is diverted around the stomach. Obesity rose to epidemic proportions while I was still in medicine. A lot of people, even many in medicine, have trouble dealing compassionately with these patients. Maybe not even on a conscious level, they see those patient's problems as self-inflicted. For me, remembering that the risk of death associated with that condition was on par with some cancers helped me to be understanding and non-judgemental toward those patients. Because St.Vincent Carmel Hospital was a bariatric center for excellence, we saw a lot of them.

The art of medicine includes demonstrating to your patients that while something is routine to you, you understand that it is not for them. I treated every one of them as important, but I told my friends that I never wanted to stitch another squirming, screaming child as long as I lived. I was over that part of the "routine." From a medical provider's point of view, diagnosing and treating someone with an unusual condition helps keep the job alive. Fortunately, there were plenty of extraordinary events there at Carmel that put some pepper in the pot. While these may just be words to non-medical observers, some of the high point moments in my entire career included diagnosing toxic shock syndrome, serum sickness, and measles (I didn't see a case until I had been in practice twenty-eight years), pulling a large plastic Easter egg out of a lady's vagina, and seeing a patient who had been bitten by a bat.

Practicing in a developed, affluent suburb of Indianapolis, I didn't expect to ever see anyone who had been bitten by a bat unless he had been spelunking. When I saw the complaint, "bat bite," posted on the computer from triage, I was expecting a story about exotic travel. No, this man had been doing yard work all day at home there in Carmel. His habit, whenever he went into his house, was to slip his shoes off and leave them in the garage. The last time he went to put his shoes back on, he felt something stick his right big toe. It felt sharp to him. He peered into his shoe expecting to find a splinter, bee, or spider. A bat squealed at him instead. Seriously? Now whenever I put on the boots that I keep in our mudroom at home, I turn them upside down and shake them first.

Unusual cases not only provided a break in the common experience, they often reminded me why I became a doctor in the first place. As with the toxic shock and serum sickness examples that I mentioned, uncommon also frequently meant much more serious. Those patients were what my extended family would have called "bad sick," and caring for really ill patients was what I envisioned a doctor to do when I was dreaming as a kid. Preventing something terrible could also be very rewarding. The guy with the bat bite potentially had an extremely dangerous situation. Rabies, a disease caused by a virus found in the saliva of certain animals, attacks the brain and is almost always fatal in humans if not treated properly. It can be transmitted to humans through a bite. Patients are always worried about getting rabies when their gerbil or the neighbor's dog bites them. That's almost never a concern. Fortunately, in the United States, the tragedy of Old Yeller and the need for Atticus Finch's heroics are things of the past. Mainly because of vaccinations, we just don't find rabies in domesticated animals in this country very often anymore. However, it's still seen in wildlife, and bats top the list. Of the one hundred twenty-seven human rabies cases in the U.S. since 1960, seventy percent have been related to exposures to bats.[4] Fortunately because of preventive medical practices, human fatalities due to rabies are extremely rare now. When I saw our patient, the bat was already in a freezer at his veterinarian's office. Until it could be tested to see if it carried rabies, we needed to start treatment to prevent the disease, and that required consultation with the Indiana State Department of Health. It was a big deal, and not trying to be overly dramatic, it could have saved this man's life.

There were many other departures from the ordinary. One impressive encounter was the case of motor oil urine. Our

---

4 https://www.cdc.gov/rabies/location/usa/index.html

nursing staff at Carmel was great. If a patient had to use the restroom, they would always instruct him or her to collect a specimen in case we needed it. I was sitting at my workstation, and I could see into a room where a patient had just been taken. A full urine specimen container was sitting on the countertop. You have seen what the used oil looks like when they drain it out of your car at the Jiffy Lube. That's what the stuff in that cup looked like. I can't remember what other doc was working that day, but I do remember that I hurried up to get to that chart first. Curiosity can be a powerful motivator. I quickly signed up to see this patient on the computer and grabbed his chart. The chief complaint was reported to be severe leg pains. This was getting stranger by the minute.

I walked into the room and extended my usual greeting. "Hi. I'm Doug Smith. I'm one of the doctors here." Then without waiting, I said as I pointed to the specimen on the counter, "Is that your motor oil there?"

My patient was a gentleman in his late fifties, and the brief levity got us off on the right foot. He grinned and said, "Yeah Doc, what about that?" We then proceeded quickly through the usual steps in an evaluation. Pretty healthy. No previous serious health problems. He had previously been very sedentary, and he decided to make a healthy lifestyle change by starting to exercise. I cannot recall the exact time frame, but he had worked out for the first time in a few years. Among other things, he did some exercises that targeted the legs. None of what he described seemed excessively strenuous. He expected to be sore, but he was experiencing severe, increasing pain in both legs. The pain got progressively worse over a couple of hours so he came to the hospital. He noticed that his urine was a little dark earlier in the day, but he thought he just needed to drink more water. He was as surprised by the specimen he provided as we were. The important points were that he was very uncomfortable, his thighs and calves on both sides were rock hard and exquisitely tender. When I moved his knees and ankles, it caused him considerable muscle pain. This man had compartment syndrome in different muscle groups in both of his legs, and he had rhabdomyolysis. Muscles are housed in little apartments we call compartments. They are surrounded by tough connective tissue that doesn't allow for a lot of swelling. When the swelling gets to be too much, it cuts off blood supply and damages nerves that go through the affected area. That can lead to disability and even the need for amputation within just a few hours. When muscles break down they release a protein called myoglobin into the bloodstream, and that gets excreted in the urine. The breakdown of the muscles is called rhabdomyolysis. Add that all together, and this man had a true emergency condition. He needed emergency surgery.

The orthopedic surgeon on call was Dr. Bruce Rougraff, a classmate of mine from medical school. He wasn't convinced. While not a zebra in a farm of horses, compartment syndrome is not all that common, and to have it occurring simultaneously in both legs, well… Still, he came right away to see this nice gentleman. By the time he got there, lab results were back.

A blood test that shows muscle injury was extremely elevated. It didn't take Dr. Rougraff long to change his mind once he saw the patient. He had him in the operating room in about twenty minutes. The procedure is called a fasciotomy in which that tough, connective tissue casing around the muscles is opened up to allow the muscles to expand and relieve the pressure. In all probability, Dr. Rougraff's quick, decisive actions prevented this guy from enduring a lifetime of debilitation. I received a note from the patient a while later. He was thanking me for my role in his treatment and letting me know that he was doing well. He even mentioned "motor oil" in the note.

Power tools had a way of adding some variety and urgency to the usual cast of injuries on display on any given day in the Emergency Department, and table saw injury was a triage description that always got my attention. One time, I saw an older man. He was retired and enjoyed woodworking. While working on one of his favorite projects, he got two fingers caught in the saw, severing them in a bloody mess. He had been making tiny, wood, pocket crosses that he would distribute to anyone he could. He gave a couple of them to me. I arranged for him to be taken care of by a hand surgeon. The mangled pieces of the digits could not be reattached, but he was treated in such a way as to make his hand as functional as it could be.

About three or four years later, the complaint posted from triage was once again "table saw injury." I saw the same gentleman, who had been doing exactly the same thing. His injuries were even worse the second time around. I appreciated his enthusiasm, but I told him he had to get a new ministry.

Plan for the Future

While not at the very end, I saw those last two patients toward the close of my career in the Express Care. Both these men were so thankful for the care we gave them. Their expressions of gratitude were extremely uplifting. Seeing those types of patients made the decision to leave a difficult one to make. I contemplated and mulled over and over an idea in my mind that just would not go away. There was something else I felt like I had to do. Ultimately, I did decide that it was time for me to leave the Emergency Department and begin to slide out of medicine altogether. It would take about a year and a half for everything to come together.

Unlike the move to Express Care from private practice years earlier, this transition was more well-planned. The details were worked out over about eighteen months before I got to the hard part. I have never been a fan of goodbyes. I emotionally attach to people I am around. My wife will tell you I am the worst of anybody at funerals. When each of our daughters left for college, Laura took it much more in stride than I did. That is just the way I am wired. So, leaving the Emergency Department, where I had worked with people, my colleagues, and friends, for many years was not easy for me. I told as few people as possible that I was leaving. On my last night there, it was still pretty busy as I was leaving. I had finished my work and stood next to the doors to the ambulance bay. I turned and said to everybody and nobody in particular, "It's been great. I thank all of you."

Nancy, one of our super unit secretaries, looked up briefly

from where she was working on her computer and said, "Good night, Dr. Smith." I walked out the door. As grueling as life often was in the Emergency Department, there was still a great deal of comfort in the routine participation in chaos and the camaraderie of exceptional, dedicated people. I would miss that, but I was on to a new and different chapter in life. Much like when I left private practice to join the emergency care group all those years before, it was exciting, exhilarating, and yes, even though it was thought out more carefully, it was just a little scary.

15

Transitioning

I attended Indiana University because I was a lunatic about its basketball team. Before we moved to Moonsville, my dad spent weeks painting and hanging shelves to create a home office that looked like the Hoosiers' locker room for me. I fell in love with basketball when I was a little kid. I remember shooting and playing games with neighborhood kids for hours on a backboard that was hung on a detached garage down the street from our house. I got into hot water with our babysitter, because I kept coming home late from school. Pickup games on the playground after school were too good to pass up. It seemed like we always had enough to play three on three and often four on four. The surface on the playground was asphalt, not cinder like at home. It was heaven. Getting in trouble for those games was worth it.

For a long time, the organized basketball of my dreams was not possible for me. I was a late bloomer. The biological information on my first driver's license had me at five feet two inches tall and weighing in at a whopping one hundred six pounds. Of course, I tried out for the school team every year including my senior year of high school, and I was disappointed every time at not making the cut. Anderson, IN has a basketball tradition as rich as anywhere in the country. The home gym of the Anderson Indians was called the Wigwam, and it was for many years the largest high school gym in the nation, with a seating capacity of 8,996. Before General Motors pulled its plants out of Anderson, the population supported three high schools. Intercity rivalry games and sectional and regional tournament games saw the Wigwam filled to standing room only, and games, players, and coaches were legendary. During my high school and college years, Indiana University was a dominant program. My high school, Madison Heights, fed Coach Knight's team several key players. There just wasn't room for a runt in the basketball world I longed to be a part of. Physical stature relegated me to the roles of casual church league and intramural player, and devout fan. I was the guy who would watch VHS tapes of IU games three or four times. I studied those games, and I knew those teams better than anybody. Through the magic of the Internet and satellite television, I was able to continue to follow Coach Knight's teams at Texas Tech. I tried to schedule the first four days of the NCAA tournament off as often as I could. In 2000, the Holy Grail, the Final Four was in Indianapolis. My wife's brother-in-law owned a slew of telecommunication stores and got some corporate passes to behind the scenes activities. He invited me to go along. Overall, it was a fantastic experience. I even had my picture taken with Dick Vitale, but the biggest highlight was a chance encounter with Mark Few, the head coach at Gonzaga.

The Bulldogs had just made an unexpected run in the tournament. I was wandering around, taking in the sights when I noticed a man standing by himself outside the booth where the Jim Rome radio show was being broadcast. It was Coach Few. He was waiting to be interviewed. I went over and congratulated him and introduced myself. We had a very brief conversation. I found him to be most gracious and humble, and I have been a fan of Mark Few and the Gonzaga program ever since.

My oldest daughter went to Butler, so of course, I became more interested in that great program. Having two Bulldog teams, Gonzaga and Butler, to cheer and study, helped quench the thirst I have for the greatest game for a few years.

It was not until my youngest daughter's junior and senior years in high school that my passion for basketball was reacquainted with the high school game. Erin attended a very small private school in Anderson called Liberty Christian. While she was there, her school enjoyed a remarkable boys team. In 2014-15, they fell one play short in the semi-state of making it to the state final. Driving home with family after that game, I told my daughter that the prospects for the following season were through the roof. Wouldn't it be great, if during her senior year she could be part of something very special? She immediately replied that she had no interest in cheerleading. I already knew that, but I had stumbled onto a scene in the short-lived television show called "Freaks and Geeks" that I had caught on Netflix. It had planted a seed in my mind. "What about mascot?" I asked her. I saw the immediate spark in her eyes, and I knew the idea was already in full blossom. She tried-out and became the mascot for the 2015-16 Lions, who came out of the gate ranked number one in the state in class 1a. I drove her to almost every game that season. Being able to watch that team and my daughter at the same time was the most gratifying experience.

The team lived up to its billing. Two of their four blemishes on the season came from teams that would ultimately win their state championships in Class 2a and Class 3a, respectively. The regional tournament still has a format in which three games are played on the same day. The early games see two teams eliminated while the winners advance to the regional championship in the evening. Some five years later, Erin and I still mark that as a day among our very favorites. We spent an entire day together doing nothing and everything at the same time. It seemed like there was a long time between games. We ate. We bowled. We laughed. We listened to our music, and we walked around downtown Frankfort, IN taking goofy pictures.

At lunch, we encountered a little girl who reminded us that no matter our situation, compassion and empathy are vital attributes. Of course, we were supporting the Lions with our attire. This girl was decked out, head to toe, in spirit wear for the team we had dispatched in the morning contest. She glared at us so intensely that it was almost comical. While we reveled in our victory, that one encounter reminded us that someone else might not have the same perspective. That thought is one that I still have to work on constantly.

We had to be conscientious about Erin's preparation for the evening game. We focused on hydrating her slight body that would be spending another hour and a half in a lion suit in the hot, crowded, raucous Case Arena of Frankfort High School. The Lion, just like the Lions, had to be ready.

The evening game pitted our Lions against Lafayette Central Catholic, a perennial powerhouse, who had a very good team that year. We were darn lucky to force the game into overtime on truly a last-second shot, and we won in that first overtime with a shot that literally bounced five times on the rim as the buzzer went off. The rest of the road to the state championship was not as bumpy. We claimed the title against Bloomfield at Bankers Life Fieldhouse in Indianapolis two weeks later. I still remember like it was yesterday. Erin had extracted herself from the lion suit and had come out of the dressing room. As she was making her way up to where our family and friends were sitting, people were trying to talk to her and congratulate her. She was having no part of it. She had predetermined her destination and nothing could slow her down. She made a beeline straight for her old dad, and we hugged in an embrace of pure joy. I have a picture of that moment on my bulletin board above my desk, but I really don't need one. That moment is permanently etched in my recall. "We did it!"

To say it was a thrill to watch that team attain the ultimate goal is an understatement, but something more was calling from some immeasurable depth inside me. I had been the guy who sat directly behind the bench all season trying to hear as much of everything as I possibly could. The players came to recognize me, and I got to know a couple of them pretty well. Similar to how it was for me and the IU teams, I had come to know as much about a team as a person could from the outside looking in, but I wanted more. I wanted to smell the ball, hear the squeak of the shoes, see the plans and drills that inspire players, and develop a team. I wanted to be part of a basketball team.

That was the "something else" I was being drawn to when I started making plans to leave the Emergency Department. I did one thing I might not have in the early years of our marriage. I talked things over with Laura, before I plowed headlong into a major life decision. I told her I wanted to be a basketball coach. Her reply was, "It's about time." The people closest to us, who really love us, might know our hearts as well or better than we do. That encouragement was all it took.

Fortunately for me, graduation that year meant that the Lions lost a ton of talent from that championship team. They would be rebuilding. At least it would not look like I was trying to squeeze in on an already elite situation. I called Jason Chappell, the head coach and athletic director at Liberty Christian, and told him I wanted to speak with him for just a minute. He tried to get me to give him some indication of what I was wanting, but I knew it would be harder for him to say no in person than over the phone. At the appointed time, I showed up in his office wearing a tie and carrying a professional resumé that had nothing to do with basketball. He knew me as Erin's dad, and he praised her for doing a great job as mascot. Then he asked what he could do for me. That's when I spit it out. "I want to be a basketball coach."

I still remember his response. He leaned back and sighed heavily, "Why?" A man whose team had just won a state championship was sincerely wondering what would possess someone to take on this role, especially in my position of life. We talked for about thirty minutes. He pointed out many of the less glamorous aspects of coaching that an outsider might not have considered, but he realized that my eagerness was not going to be deflated. Finally, he said he would think about taking me on as a volunteer coach, and he gave me a couple of internet links that dealt with the tactics the team used on offense and defense.

I was ecstatic. I reveled in studying the resources he gave me. I showed up to as many summer workouts as my schedule would allow. That summer and the regular season that followed, I was still working with the St. Vincent group. My friend, Dr. Mary Reilly, who made the schedule for our group, worked with me so that I only missed a couple of varsity games that first season. I made over half the practices. After that, the hook was set deeply. Every little detail of the gym, the workouts, the players, the interactions among all the pieces was more than I had imagined. I made the decision to leave St. Vincent Emergency Physicians to be able to work part-time for a company called Activate Healthcare. That allowed me to make all the practices and games. Trade: full-time physician, part-time coach — full-time coach, part-time physician.

I enjoyed many benefits from being a medical professional over the years, not the least of which was job security. My family's financial stability never waivered during the 2008 financial crisis. When I decided that I wanted to move on from St.V, I answered one headhunter. I was flooded with more than a thousand solicitations to fill all kinds of positions including several from outside the United States. I couldn't keep up with my inbox. Fortunately, one of the earliest that I saw was an intriguing opportunity to participate in a model for the delivery of primary care that I had read about but had not seen first hand. Activate Healthcare was a company that contracted with businesses to provide medical care for their employees at a discounted rate. They were in need of a physician for a clinic in Elwood, IN, which is just twenty minutes from my driveway. Their primary customer at that site was Red Gold, a well-respected company that grows, develops, packages, and distributes all manner of top-notch tomato products all over the world. It turned out our needs were well matched. The interview process was painless. I would only agree to part-time work that allowed me to leave no later than 2 p.m., so I could make practice every day. They really only wanted a part-time physician. The people at Red Gold were the kind of down-to-earth, straightforward people I enjoyed serving the most. I had an arrangement in place before I left the Emergency Department. I think I was "unemployed" for two weeks.

It may not seem like it to most people, but transitioning back into primary care from urgent, emergency care was a big deal. The approach is radically different. I had to readjust my thinking and my study habits. I had always taken pride in staying up to date in my continuing medical education, but for almost twenty-two years I had focused my efforts mainly on emergency care. I spent the interim two weeks cramming as much information as I could about managing the typical problems that one encounters in a primary care office setting. Yes, I had done this before, but things had changed drastically over all those years. Yes, it was a little like riding a bicycle. I had tremendous Internet resources at my disposal and colleagues at Activate who were graciously willing to consult with me if needed. Yet, if I am honest, I still felt just a little apprehension. I didn't experience the full-blown self-doubt that plagued me earlier in my career, but I still had to work out a little anxiety.

Fate again, God's intervention? Whatever we call it, I was again extremely fortunate. I found some fantastic support to aid me in the transition. Theresa was the nurse practitioner who essentially had been working the clinic for over a year by herself. Until I arrived, she had been collaborating with a physician off-site. She was clearly relieved to have some in-person support, and I quickly recognized that she was the consummate medical professional. She was dedicated, caring, and always eager to learn. In one respect, she reminded me of myself at the start of my career. She was Type A and compulsive. Besides sharing what I could about diagnoses, acute care management, EKG interpretation, and the like, I started planting the seeds that she needed to be kind to herself. Funny how much easier it is to see things in others than in ourselves. Pursuing excellence is good, but I have already relayed how trying to be perfect was almost the complete undoing of my career. I didn't want to see her go down that road strewn with those gigantic potholes.

I think out of some weird sense of respect, she pretended not to notice that I learned as much from her as she did from me. She was particularly gracious in guiding me through dealing with a most cumbersome computer system.

We had a team relationship. We reviewed diagnosis and treatment strategies. Staying sharp was important because just like the urgent care setting, the office can be a set-up for becoming mentally stagnant and ill-prepared for recognizing and dealing with more serious problems. Steadily dealing every day with diabetes, high blood pressure, cholesterol issues, depression, osteoarthritis, and seasonal respiratory infections could be as hypnotizing as driving on the highway. More than a little pathology tried to catch us with our heads turned. I recall a laundry list of more serious problems we saw during my time at Activate that included an anaphylactic (severe allergic) reaction, a ruptured diverticulum (hole in the colon), profound hypothyroidism (severely underactive thyroid gland), and chronic carbon monoxide poisoning. Once again, what doctor Walker had taught me all of those years ago was proving to be true to the very end. Pathology was always lurking, waiting to find a medical practitioner unaware. Having to be alert, to be able to care for patients who were acutely ill, was what kept some excitement in medicine for me until I finally called it quits.

16

Hillary

Theresa was the first to leave Activate. Ultimately, it was the impossibly wide breadth of primary care and some administrative hassles that were weighing on her too heavily. She was able to land a position that allowed her to narrow her focus to diabetes management, and her commute was cut in half. I was happy for her, but it nearly killed me. Although never formally labeled as such, I was losing my role as mentor. Teaching and acquiring knowledge with motivated learners was something that I had really enjoyed over the years, and I knew when Theresa left that was the end of that part of my career. I turned in my letter of resignation shortly after Theresa moved on. People around me kept saying I was retiring. To me, that wasn't exactly correct. I just quit. From a financial standpoint, it was probably a year too early that I rode off into the sunset, but continuing on without my wing woman and dealing with a computer system that just did not work one or two times a week frustrated me enough to cause me to pull the trigger.

I'm not completely anti-computer. I get that it would be ideal for patients to have permanent, mobile medical records that follow them wherever they go for care. Right now that interface is just not there. Records are not currently shared across systems. There are a couple more problems with the computer. As I mentioned, they don't always work, and when the waiting room is full of patients who value their time, that's an issue. At St.Vincent, we were a little late in adopting computerized records. Not too long after our first system was up and running, Dr. Steve Purdy, a medical staff administrator came through the E.D.

"How's it going with the computer?" he asked me.

"Well, it slows me down, and I make more mistakes."

"Yeah, that's consistent with the national statistics."

What the heck? I don't know any physician who wants to be slower and more error-prone. I definitely don't know any patient who desires that for his or her doctor. Additionally, physicians, almost universally, resent the time they have to spend in tedious data entry. They want to be face to face, providing care for their patients, not their "clients."

The depersonalization of care with the computer is just one factor that made medicine less appealing than it had been back in what older doctors referred to as the golden age of medicine. In the past, a physician might happily stay in one practice location, often the same building, for forty years, but times have changed. There is at least one major battlefield modern-day practitioners have to navigate that those elder statesmen of yesteryear did not endure. Today, physicians find themselves constantly engaged in combat with ding-dang, blasted insurance companies. Practicing in the Emergency Department for so many years, I was mostly insulated from these knock-down, drag-out fights. Precertification for emergency care was almost never required. At Activate, I got reintroduced to that whole process very quickly. About once a week, my staff would have to request an appeal to have a procedure, diagnostic study, or medication I prescribed covered by the patient's insurance. Almost always the can was kicked down the road, and I would have to speak with a nurse or physician reviewer myself. Each of those reviews took twenty to forty-five minutes. Especially since not one, not a single one, of my personal appeals was ever denied, I considered that entire exercise a colossal waste of time and energy. I could have spent that time with my patients.

I consider myself to be in the "tweener" stage. I started as the golden age was coming to a close, and young doctors today have never known medicine without computers and insurance red tape. Change is an inevitable part of life, and so much of dealing with change is attitude. I understand that many of us have a tendency to glorify the past. I also firmly believe that when dealing with something as important as the delivery of healthcare, it is incumbent upon us to assess critically whether or not change has been for the good. For doctors, and more importantly, for patients, I'm not so sure these changes have been beneficial. Considering the direction medicine was moving helped me decide to shut it all down. It was just time for me to coach.

During my exit, I tried to be as helpful to Activate and our patients there as I could be. The administration asked me to meet with prospective new hires, and I was happy to do so. While participating in these interviews, I was reminded of how small and close-knit the medical community could be. A couple of doctors came through. The last turned out to be someone I had known in years past. Dr. Heather Gutwein had been a student on a few rotations with me when I was a resident at St. Vincent. As a student, she had been superb. We had a great talk. I was able to give a hearty thumbs up to Activate, and they already seemed to like her. After they hired her, we overlapped for a short while as I was working out my contract. Spending more time with her made me sense even more that she would be a good fit for the clinic and that patients would be well cared for. That made me feel better about leaving.

I also met with nurse practitioners who were looking to possibly fill Theresa's spot. One day as the work in my chosen profession was truly coming to an end, Jason Vore, one of the admins at Activate was showing a prospective candidate around. He stepped into my office and said, "I want to introduce you…", but he was cut off. The person he was interviewing was someone else I had known many years in the past. Kerry was a nurse I worked with during my third year as a resident when I was moonlighting in the Emergency Department at Mercy Hospital there in Elwood. I hadn't seen Kerry in a very long time. Both our eyes lit up, and we gave a collective, "Hey" in unison. Then we went right past the handshake and hugged. Somewhat astonished, Jason said, "I guess you two already know each other."

Bob Helm was two years ahead of me in training. He helped me a lot when we were at Ball Memorial, and we kept in contact after I defected from Ball to St.Vincent. When he graduated from the Family Medicine program at Ball, he had his private practice, and he directed the moonlighting program to staff the Emergency Department there at Mercy Hospital on nights and weekends. He gave me the opportunity to work there during my last year as a resident. Call was almost non-existent for a third-year resident, so I could supplement my income and experience by working at Mercy one or two times a week. During the week it was 6 p.m. to 6 a.m. On the weekends, it was 6 a.m. to 6 a.m. My main incentive was financial; it was how I raised the money to pay for Laura's engagement ring. Laura and Kerry knew each other from nursing school, so Kerry was supportive of my secret motive.

Kerry was not the only nurse with whom I worked. It just seemed like our shifts matched up frequently. I don't want to gloss over the valuable experience part of the equation. That time was spent in vulnerable, formative periods for both of us. She was a young nurse who had skills and savvy way beyond her years. I was a third-year Family Medicine resident who was crazy enough to work solo coverage in an emergency department. Mercy had a small hospital emergency room in a small, blue-collar town. Most of the time was pretty quiet. The cases were more urgent, less emergent, but there were crazy moments of terror that ripped through the calm. In terms of physician support, there was none. Almost always, there wasn't even another doctor in the building. I remember when I intubated a patient for the first time without anyone around to bail me out if I was unsuccessful. Relief washed over the two of us when the tube was accurately placed on the first try. There would be more intubations, and there would be plenty of fresh new experiences for the uninitiated. Kerry helped me the first time I relocated a dislocated shoulder. We were on shift together when the ambulance brought in a sixteen-year-old girl who had a sixteen-week fetus hanging out between blood-covered thighs. We cared for a few heart attack victims, and there was the victim of the self-inflicted gunshot wound to the ear canal who could still carry on a conversation with us. Surviving those kinds of experiences together, while running around naive and green, has a way of forging a special bond. We came to trust and respect one another, and we became friends.

Jason could tell we needed to catch up, and he left us for a few minutes. We didn't rehash those old cases. She wanted to know how Laura was able to put up with me for all those years. We described the current conditions of our respective families. She had been working as a nurse practitioner in Dr. Helm's office for many years. She was just timidly exploring possibilities for a change. She was curious to know why I was bailing out.

It really was only a few minutes that we had. Knowing that Jason would be coming back soon, I asked Kerry, "Do you remember...?"

"Hillary," she said before I could finish, and her eyes pooled ever so slightly revealing grief that had long been repressed.

Back in the day when I wasn't seeing patients there at Mercy, there was a call room where I would hang out. I could read, watch television, or sleep if I wanted to. It was late one night somewhere around midnight. Isn't that when all stories, good and bad, seem to unfold? The ringing of the phone pierced the night. "What you got?" I asked while the cobwebs of sleep still clouded my consciousness.

"Doug, I need you down here."

Alarmed by Kerry's tone, I queried her as I was pulling on my shoes. "What is it?"

"Sick baby," and she hung up.

Foreboding dread stifled my breathing as I ran down the stairs and through the hallway to get to the Emergency Room. When I arrived, I found Kerry on one side of a child, probably five to six years old. There lay this beautiful brown-haired, brown-eyed, slight, little girl who was literally as white as the sheet on which she was lying. She was offering no resistance as Kerry was attempting to start an IV in her left arm. She was indeed a "sick baby." I took up a position on the right side trying to find a suitable site for an IV. As Kerry looked on the left and I on the right, I got caught up on the history and physical that had been obtained so far. Kerry gave me most of the information and the rest was provided by terrified parents who held onto each other as they leaned against one of the walls there in the Trauma Room. Her blood pressure was a little low. Heart rate was just a little fast. Breathing was a little fast but not labored. Her oxygen levels were normal. Her rectal temperature was below normal. She had previously been healthy. Fully immunized. No recent travel. No known exposures to poisons, toxins, or sick people. She had a very mild runny nose for a couple of days. Her mom was getting ready to go to bed when she checked on Hillary and found her in this condition. They brought her straight to the Emergency Department.

Signs pointed to an overwhelming infection, possibly meningitis. Staying true to our training, we each only tried the one time for an IV. We did not waste time. As Kerry was reaching for our next alternative, an intraosseous needle, one that actually goes into a bone, words of Dr. Anne Eliades popped into my head. "Look at the neck." Dr. Eliades was a staff pediatrician at Ball Hospital. I had spent time with her when I was an intern. She was known for chewing up and spitting out house staff, and of course, I really liked her. She told us to take just a second to look at the neck for a vein before we resorted to the intraosseous or the next step, a central line - an IV in one of the big deep inside veins at different places in the body. Sure enough, the way Hillary was lying exposed a visible external vein in her neck, and I was able to quickly get an intravenous catheter in place that flowed freely. We were able to quickly give her a bolus of fluids and antibiotics that would cover a broad range of possible bacterial germs.

Here is one place my recollection gets fuzzy. I can't remember why, but we were unable to transfer her to Riley Children's Hospital. It may be that they had no available beds. I spoke to a resident in the Emergency Department at Methodist Hospital. He was a classmate from medical school, and he agreed to our transfer. As we waited for the transport team, I took more history and examined Hillary thoroughly from head to toe. I was searching for clues that never presented themselves. Again with no resistance, Kerry put a catheter in her bladder. A urine specimen would be sent to the lab, and the catheter offered a way to accurately monitor urine output.

Finally, our welcome relief arrived. They were experts in pediatrics, and they were used to seeing really sick children. They approved of everything we had done except they did not like the IV site. I certainly wanted anything and everything that could be done for that critically ill child, but somehow in a weird way, it made me feel good that the experts weren't able to find a different peripheral IV site either. When Hillary left our little ER, the only functioning IV she had was the one we had placed in her neck a couple of hours earlier.

About three or four days later, Kerry called me at St. Vincent to let me know that Hillary had died.

Subsequently, we would learn that an autopsy failed to demonstrate a definite cause of death. For a long time after that, I would see Hillary at the most unexpected times, in the most unexpected places. Her curls framed beautiful doe-like eyes that would look out of the mirror at me as I brushed my teeth, and the entire scene from the Emergency Room seemed always to accompany me on all drives of any distance. Fortunately, time did apply its healing salve and those vivid pictures and memories did fade. There has to be some irony in the fact that some thirty years later in the very last days of my medical career I should have a chance encounter with one of my favorite people in medicine and that it should trigger once again those visions, not of a case in the Emergency Department, but of a precious life lost despite our very best efforts.

That day in the Activate office, Kerry said, "Dr. Alexander," a colleague of ours, "always said it had to be meningitis." As Mr. Vore rejoined us, I just cleared my throat and turned the conversation back to good luck and so long.

Epilogue

This manuscript is by no means a complete record of all that transpired during my life in and around clinical medicine. Many days were pretty uneventful and even forgettable. Others left indelible marks on my memory. One time, I saw a college kid at one of the hospitals where I worked. He was home for the holiday break between semesters. The triage complaint was pain in the groin. His mother accompanied him, and when I entered the exam room, he asked her to leave. He wasted no time or words in revealing his situation to me. He had a limp because he had pain in the groin. He had pain in the groin because his right testicle and scrotum were swollen and black. His testicle and scrotum were swollen and back because they had been entrapped in a device called a "cock and ball ring" for a little over two weeks.

Approximately fifteen days before I saw him, he had been wearing this device and sitting in front of his computer when his roommate and friends surprised him. He was not expecting them, but he was able to conceal his activity. Now, this is the great mystery. Why he didn't simply excuse himself to the restroom and remove the contraption before he went out drinking with his pals, heaven only knows. By the time he woke up late the next afternoon the right scrotum and testicle were swollen, and he couldn't remove the ring. Although the left testicle and penis were also encased in the apparatus, the fit was such that only the right side got pinched. Swelling continued to increase. Blood supply to the area was cut off, and his testicle and scrotum had become a mass of dry gangrene (putrefying but not draining pus). This young man was letting his scrotum and testicle rot because he had been too embarrassed to ask for help. He was treated by Urology and underwent a couple operations that included orchiectomy (removal of the testicle).

That story is representative of the types of events that seem to intrigue non-medical people looking for anecdotes from clinical life. While these memories really do loom like a sensational highlight reel, they are, thankfully, only a fraction of the actual time spent in the practice of medicine. Something the non-medical person usually does not consider is that, while snippets such as this one certainly are sensational, they each make a little withdrawal from the provider's emotional bank account. That young man, really just a kid, let that word sink in - *kid*, was sick. Another aspect of those events is that they leave the more sensitive among us pondering. What in the totality of the human experience can make it even remotely possible that something like that could happen? That is why most doctors I know are truly grateful that these fantastic vignettes really are infrequent.

As I am concluding this project, I have just completed an unexpected detour in life by finishing up a year of teaching middle school science and high school biology, and we are in the middle of the Covid-19 pandemic. I halfway expected that my old group might reach out for me to dust off the stethoscope and return to help. Fortunately, the Indianapolis area has not been completely overwhelmed as other regions of the world have been. They didn't ask, and I didn't volunteer. I have reached out to a few of my friends to offer support and encouragement. They are hanging tough, and I pray for them all the time.

Even before this crisis, medicine was proceeding in its ceaseless advance. Just as there was a sense of irony for me remembering Hillary at the end of my career, I find the same in considering that one of the most exciting areas in medicine today is the exploding field of genetic engineering. Viruses, as we now know all too well, can obviously be deadly, but there may be some viruses that can be used to deliver targeted treatments for conditions such as cancer. The landscape of medical problems, illnesses, and maladies cured and emerging will be forever changing, and thankfully there will always be doctors who are willing to fight the good fight.

As for my situation, I know I landed exactly where I am meant to be. Coaching is a full-time job and then some. Just as with medicine, or any position for that matter, there are facets of the job description that aren't obvious from the outside looking in. Driving kids to and from practice, driving the "people mover" to games, sweeping the floor, airing up balls, taping ankles, late meals after road games are some of the less obvious parts of the job, and I love all of it. Even though I entered this field pretty much a blank sheet, I haven't fallen prey to Impostor Syndrome. I think two factors helped me stave off the self-doubt of old. I already learned many lessons from that great instructor, experience, and I came under the tutelage of the greatest mentors. Our Head Coach, Jason Chappell, has put up with my basketball all the time mentality, and Coach Mike Carey is the coach's coach. He has guided me with expertise and unbelievable patience. The first lesson taught was that systems and strategies are just small parts of basketball. Helping players to harness the ability to be self-motivated, to control their emotions, to develop a growth mindset, to work in a team setting, to see that attention to process is what generally leads to the desired outcome, is the true art of coaching. I wish that I had learned these lessons when I was young. They're applicable to all aspects of life, not just basketball. I apply techniques that we teach the kids for mastering the mental game in my daily life all the time now. Maybe, if I had this arsenal for fostering cognitive and emotional maturity when I was first in practice, I wouldn't have made everyone around me miserable while I was running around trying to be perfect.

In keeping with a concept I have already hit on a couple of times, basketball isn't all good either. We've had some good play and some bad play. I've seen players do some really cool things off the court in service to others, and I've seen a few do things I wish they hadn't. Players have graduated and gone on to big things— attending college, playing in college, and careers outside of sports. A few have left the program under other circumstances. Three players who weren't able to complete playing careers with us have still left marks on our hearts. One took his own life, another died amidst the Covid pandemic, and the last of those three is incarcerated. Existing in this cosmos continually bombards us with circumstances that revolve around everything we do, including basketball, and those situations are never all good or all bad. Right now, I just can't envision myself living life with all that goes with it, anywhere except in association with a basketball team.

Coaching basketball is where I am currently, but I can't help reminiscing about medicine some. As I indicated previously, grouping or mapping is an aspect of memory that I find interesting. The concept occurred to me again as I was thinking of a colleague from my earliest days in private practice. It is with the cluster of mental images I have of Dr. Stan Kepner that I want to leave you. Dr. Kepner was an old pediatrician who practiced in Anderson for years. Whenever a snapshot of him flashes in my mind, it is immediately accompanied by two bullet points - crotchety demeanor and sage advice. He was an excellent clinician, and he could be just a little irritable. Occasionally, he went out of his way to give me advice, and I always found it to be sound. Once, early in my career, I was all fired up about some hospital management issue. I was ranting in the doctors' lounge about how I was going to write a letter and say this and that. As I was walking out the door of the lounge, Dr. Kepner was behind me, and he grabbed me by the back of the neck and steered me to the side of the hallway. "Smitty," he said, "write that poison pen letter and stick it in a drawer. Take it out three days from now. If you still feel the same, send it." I did as he said, and I ended up not sending the letter. Another piece of counsel he gave me was this. "Don't believe it when somebody tells you that you are the greatest thing since sliced bread, because if you do, you'll also have to believe the next person who tells you that you are lower than whale shit on the bottom of the ocean."

I have never forgotten those two things Dr. Kepner taught me, but fighting self-deception is not easy for any of us. I am as guilty as anybody for allowing its charade. If I am honest with myself, I have to admit I cherish more the memories of praise and they share a more prominent place in the recesses of my mind than those of reproach.

We do tend to suppress, unconsciously if not consciously, the "whale shit" moments. Those less appealing impressions are the ones that hurt our pride. I fully realize now that I was not the "perfect" doctor. I made plenty of mistakes, and not everyone I treated was in love with me. I was fired by a few patients over the years, and I had a small number of complaints about services rendered in the Emergency Department. Some people just didn't like me or my staff. Sometimes my recommendations did not result in the cure that we hoped for, and some people did not want to pay their bills. I took those complaints very personally in the early years, but I eventually came to realize it was something that was just going to happen. I simply was not going to be able to please or even help everyone I treated.

In the biased restructuring of the events of my life practicing medicine, I do have one ego preserving mechanism. I don't see that I ever had a flippant, dismissive attitude toward my patients and their problems. Most meaningful to me, in assessing my performance over the years, is the informed opinions of colleagues and consultants with whom I worked. I hope that any and all of them would say that the shortcomings I did have were not the result of less than genuine effort. I hope they would say I was not lazy.

As for the "sliced bread," I was bestowed with plenty of accolades over the years. A few doctors asked me to care for their families when I was in private practice. I was elected President of the Medical Staff for a term. I was the subject of a newspaper article after one of my Family Medicine recertification exams. As a family doctor, I was asked to lecture at a few emergency medicine conferences. My mentor, Dr. Kelly Chambers, told me a couple of times that I was the only person he ever considered asking to join him in practice. Dr. Walker from the urgent care where I worked as a medical student called me when I was a third-year resident and offered me a job. Dr. Bill Tierney, one of the best surgeons I have ever known, went unsolicited on my behalf to the administration of the hospital when I was moving from that first practice setting in Summitville. He wanted to make sure that I did not move to another hospital. My Emergency Room group threw a magnificent, surprise, going away party for me when I left. Many students and residents asked me to write letters of recommendation for them, and most pleasing of all, I have a shoebox in the top of my closet that contains several notes and cards from patients who expressed heartfelt gratitude for what we were able to do for them.

Dr. John Woodall and I used to be the two doctors to make rounds earliest in the morning when I was in private practice. He was unaware that I had already made plans to start with St. Vincent Emergency Physicians when he stopped me in the hallway early one morning. "Hey, you want to blow everybody's mind?" he asked abruptly out of the blue. "Let's join practices." He is black, and I am white. We practiced in a town with a history of racial tensions. As I am writing, our country is being rocked with protests and calls for social reform and improved race relations. I am still honored that Dr. Woodall showed me the respect, years before it would be the popular thing to do, to consider neglecting race to join forces and practice medicine together.

In the end, despite Dr. Kepner's admonition, I think I am going to continue to allow the yang just a little more audience than the yin in my own, personal mental cache. Cognitive preservation? Perhaps, but it just feels right to me to keep the scales balanced that way. I'm not actively trying to completely wipe out the less appealing memories that hopefully I have learned from. I'm just going to hold a little tighter to the good ones.

There is one more mental highlight that I associate with Dr. Kepner, and that, of course, is one amazing patient encounter. I think it was my second or third year in private practice. It was the height of the flu season in winter, and I had been on call all weekend. I had just watched the end of a basketball game. I was tired, and I was getting ready for bed on Sunday night. The answering service called. I had a call from the ER. Dr. Jack Brown was an excellent emergency physician. He sounded a little stressed when I talked to him that night. "Doug, we're covered up here. Your partner has a six-month-old (patient) here. He is sick. I don't have time to figure it out. I need you to decide on his disposition." Click. I knew Dr. Brown well, so I knew he was truly covered up and that I would indeed be seeing another sick baby.

I arrived in the ER minutes later. Dr. Brown told me where to find the kid and that labs had been drawn. When I walked to his bed, once again, I found another limp, pale child. His dad was standing beside the bed. As I examined him, his dad relayed his history. Generally healthy. Two days of just not being himself. Crying more than usual. Not feeding well. That evening he wouldn't take a bottle at all, and he developed a fever. He was coughing a little.

Fortunately, babies and young children can be checked out thoroughly from head to toe with exposed skin in just a couple of minutes. He didn't fight me at all. His ears, nose, throat, heart, lungs, and joints were normal. Other than being pale, his skin was unremarkable. He showed no reaction when I moved his neck in every direction. As I paused just for a second to think, he turned his head back to face his dad. When he did, I saw something I hadn't previously noticed. There on the sheet next to his mouth was a little green spot about the size of my thumbnail. I pointed to it, and his dad said, "That's what he's been coughing up."

"Coughing?" I asked.

"Well, he sort of gags it."

"Gags it," I repeated, as I leaned in to get a closer look. "Bile!" I blurted. There was a bile stain on the sheet next to his mouth. Bile has a distinct green-brown color, and it comes from the liver, the gallbladder, the gastrointestinal system. I checked his belly again. It was soft everywhere except in the right lower quadrant, and he would whimper a little when I pressed there. His dad and I looked at one another. What was going on?

This child had appendicitis or some other very serious problem in his abdomen, but appendicitis is so rare in children his age that I had doubts. It was still early in my career. Could I be right about this? I didn't deliberate long. I called Dr. Kepner. He was tired, too. He had been on call all weekend as well. He grumpily voiced all the reasons why this could not be a case of appendicitis, but begrudgingly he agreed to come see the kid with me. When he arrived, he was impressed with the evidence at hand. This is probably not how the evaluation would go today, but we shot a quick x-ray that covered our patient's chest, abdomen, and pelvis. Dr. Joe Porcaro was the radiologist who was reading films that night. He showed us what looked like a baseball-sized mass in the child's right lower abdomen. He was transferred to Riley Children's Hospital in Indianapolis where he was definitively diagnosed and treated for a ruptured appendix. The last I heard that kid did great.

In the middle of an influenza outbreak, we saw a six-month-old with an abscess in his abdomen caused by an appendix that had burst open. I can't explain how beyond unbelievable that is. Dr. Kepner and I really didn't say much to each other after the kid was packaged and sent on his way. In the doctors' lounge the next morning, we presented the case to the amazement of our colleagues. All Dr. Kepner said to me was that I would never see another case like that. He was right. I never did.

Up to this point, I have demonstrated contrasts, even contradictions about my life as a doctor. I lived almost simultaneously with self-doubt and high achievement. Being on call was great for learning, and it was miserable. Practice had long mundane periods separated by the most thrilling and sometimes terrifying experiences imaginable. Those strange cases kept the excitement in medicine for me, and I was glad they didn't happen often. I lived with joy and faced heartache at the same time. In all, it truly has been an awful and wonderful life. In the tug of war between those last two extremes, a margin of victory, no less than Secretariat's epic win in the Belmont, really does go to the wonderful side. That's why I chose to relay that last case at the end of this book. I'm going to remember that I made a difference in somebody's life.

Acknowledgments

How do I begin? I'm not sure I have adequate words to express the deep gratitude I feel for the support, encouragement, and love I have received from so many.

Julie Weaver truly has the patience of Job. Her edits were on point and delivered with kindness.

Dr. Louis Profeta has been a Godsend for me. I will never forget the way he assisted me when I changed from Primary Care to Urgent Care/Emergency Medicine. His help with this book was invaluable, although his edits were not administered the same way Ms. Weaver's were.

David Provolo made me unafraid that people would judge my book by its cover.

Marty Carey and Erin Smith cleaned up my grammatical messes. I love you, you red pen monsters.

To all the teachers, formal and informal, whoever taught me anything, I can never thank you enough.

I mentioned a few by name in the body of this book, but there are hundreds more classmates from medical school, fellow interns and residents, colleagues, and consultants who took this trip with me. I shared many of my personal struggles, and I know a lot of the people I rubbed elbows with along the way had similar and even more massive mountains to climb. I am impressed by and so very thankful for the fantastic examples of determination, fortitude, and professionalism that those I surrounded myself with gave me. I have witnessed, first hand, the difference you have made in the lives of millions of people.

Sue (mom), Junior (dad), Debbie (sister), and Tommy (brother), we have come a long way. Without your influence, I would never have come to realize that the simplest things in life are the most important.

Author's Biography

J. Douglas Smith, M.D. (Dr. Smith/Coach Smith) was born and raised in Anderson, IN. He attended Indiana University for undergraduate studies and medical school. He has been Board Certified in Family Medicine since he completed his residency training at St.Vincent Hospital in Indianapolis, IN in 1989. With his wife, Laura, and two daughters, Jeri and Erin, he lives outside Anderson in what he calls the middle of a postcard in Moonsville, IN. His passions include his family, being the best friend he can be, glorifying God by doing the next right thing, and oh yeah… he sort of likes basketball.

CPSIA information can be obtained
at www.ICGtesting.com
Printed in the USA
BVHW040314011220
594588BV00019B/982